The Completely SKEWERED-UP COOKBOOK

by *IRVING J. LEVINSON*
Illustrated by JOHN A. DAVENPORT

PRENTICE-HALL, INC.
Englewood Cliffs, N.J.

The Completely Skewered-Up Cookbook
By Irving J. Levinson, Illustrated by John Davenport
Copyright © 1973 by Irving J. Levinson

Printed in the United States of America

Prentice-Hall International, Inc., London
Prentice-Hall of Australia, Pty. Ltd., North Sydney
Prentice-Hall of Canada, Ltd., Toronto
Prentice-Hall of India Private Ltd., New Delhi
Prentice-Hall of Japan, Inc., Tokyo

Library of Congress Cataloging in Publication Data

Levinson, Irving J.
The completely skewered-up cook book.

1. Cookery. 2. Broiling. I. Title. II. Title:
Skewered-up cook book.
TX715.L662 641.7'6 72-6567
ISBN 0-13-164848-9

Firstly — Good cooking is a creative art—a memorable meal is like a once seen piece of fine sculpture or a once heard delightful concerto—thoughts of the occasion linger for a long, long time.

Cooking en brochette is more a matter of technique than pharmaceutical precision or culinary finesse; it challenges the cook to try tasty and appealing variations—limited only by imagination. Any food, meat or vegetable, fish or fowl, that can be cut into bite size chunks and stuck on a stick, is fair game for Skewered-Up cooking. Liquids—soup, salad dressing, wines and liquors—that can be mixed without curdling are starting points for sauces that can be prepared in minutes and hold their own against the classic French sauces that are watched over while simmering for hours.

Skewers, plain and fancy, long and short, are easily found. Butcher skewers, pointed wooden sticks about an eighth of an inch in diameter and five inches long, are available for the asking at meat counters. Bamboo skewers, available from food specialty shops, are about ten inches long and thinner than butcher skewers; they can be snipped to any length to fit plates, platters or pans. Fancy metal skewers, also available at specialty shops, supermarket gadget racks, hardware stores, and your Syrian grandmother's, can, of course, be used, but they have their drawbacks—they can be hot to handle and they must be washed. They may even be too long to fit into your broiler. There is nothing to stop the skewer addict from practicing his craft on the oldest medium of all— the peeled green stick—indoors or out. Remember, however, that there are poisonous plants around, so never use any plant that is unknown to you.

Now, on with the cooking (Skewered-Up, of course) . . .

CONTENTS

DIRECTIONS

1. a. Color the skewer bamboo yellow.
   b. "   "   Burgundy wine burgundy.
   c. "   "   shrimp tasty pink.
   d. "   "   cherry tomatoes luscious red.
   e. "   "   olives shiny black and olive green.
   f. "   "   mushrooms succulent white.
   g. "   "   spices various flavorful colors.
2. Carefully cut out (a) through (g) on the dotted lines.
3. Arrange all possible combinations of (b) through (g) on (a) to arrive at 2,047 different recipes.*

_____   _____   _____

_____   _____   _____

_____   _____   _____

_____   _____   _____

_____   _____   _____

_____   _____   _____

_____   _____   _____

_____   _____   _____

_____   _____   _____

_____   _____   _____

*Hint: Start with shrimp, shrimp, shrimp, and you will have only 2,046 to go.

TEST YOUR ABILITY TO SKEWER-UP A COLORFUL MEAL

a.

b.

c.

d.

e.

f.

g.

BURGUNDY WINE

S

P

PAPRIKA

BAY LEAVES

OREGANO

''Doth not the appetite alter?''
SHAKESPEARE

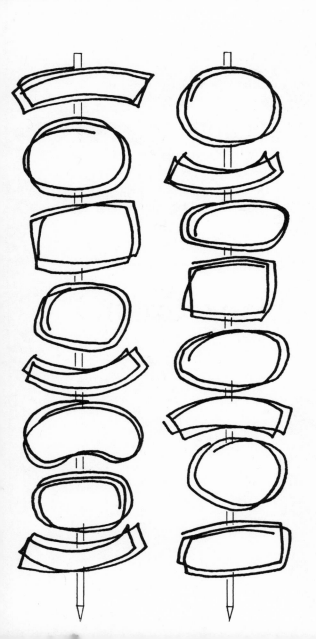

MEAT

LONDON BROIL EN BROCHETTE

Flank steak
Rosé wine
Smoked salt
Pepper
Rosemary
Garlic salt
Pitted black olives

Cut 2 pounds of flank steak diagonally across the grain of the meat into 1-inch wide strips.

Marinate the steak in the refrigerator for 4 hours in a mixture of 2 cups rosé wine, 1 teaspoon smoked salt, ¼ teaspoon pepper, ½ teaspoon dried rosemary, and ¼ teaspoon garlic salt.

Fold the steak and alternate with pitted black olives on each of 8 butcher skewers; grill over hot charcoal or oven broil for 5 minutes on each of the four sides or until done to taste.

Serves 4

Serve with foil-baked potatoes.

Flank Steak

Black Olive

STEAK MARSEILLE

Steak (sirloin, round, or lean chuck)
Mushrooms, 20 whole fresh
Butter
Green onions
Worcestershire sauce
Dry mustard
Salt, pepper, MSG
Cognac

Serves 4

Cut 2½ pounds of ¾- to 1-inch thick tender beefsteak into 1-inch squares.

Alternate mushroom caps and steak on each of 8 butcher skewers.

Sauté skewers quickly on all four sides in 3 tablespoons hot browned butter. Remove to a warmed platter.

In the same skillet, add ½ cup chopped green onions and ½ cup mushroom stems, 1½ tablespoons Worcestershire sauce, 2 teaspoons dry mustard, dash of salt, dash of fresh cracked pepper, 1 teaspoon MSG; sauté until brown.

Return the steak to the skillet and cook in the sauce for 10 minutes; turn frequently.

Preheat ¼ cup Cognac; pour over the steak and ignite.

Serve with sauce from pan and garnish with parsley.

Mushroom Cap

Steak

BUTTER

COGNAC

SKEWERED ENGLISH BEEFSTEAK WITH MUSHROOM SAUCE

Steak (sirloin, round, or lean chuck)
Mushrooms, 20 whole fresh
Butter
Green onions
Rosé wine
Tarragon
Salt, pepper

Cut a 2-pound, ¾-inch thick steak into 1-inch chunks and alternate steak and mushroom caps on each of 8 butcher skewers.

Sauté in a small amount of butter over high heat. When cooked to taste, remove to a hot platter.

Add to the skillet 4 green onions (with stems) cut into 1-inch sections, 1 cup rosé wine, ⅛ teaspoon tarragon, and the stems of the mushroom caps, finely chopped. Season with salt and freshly cracked pepper; simmer for about 10 minutes.

Add 2 tablespoons butter to the skillet and bring the sauce to a rapid boil. Return the skewers to the skillet and cook for no longer than 2 minutes.

Serves 4

Serve on triangles of toast spooned over with hot sauce from skillet.

Mushroom Cap

Steak

4

FINNISH BEEFSTEAK IN LEMON SAUCE

Steak (sirloin, rib, or lean chuck)
Mushroom caps (fresh or canned)
Flour
Paprika, salt, pepper
Basil
Peanut oil
Red onion
Dry mustard
Water
Lemon juice

Cut a ¾-inch thick steak into 1-inch chunks and thread on each of 8 butcher skewers, alternating each piece of steak with a large mushroom cap.

Dust the skewers with 1 cup flour seasoned with ½ teaspoon salt, ½ teaspoon cracked pepper, ¼ teaspoon paprika, and ¼ teaspoon basil. Reserve 3 tablespoons seasoned flour.

Sauté the skewers in hot oil for 5 minutes on each side or until the meat is crusty brown. Remove to a warm platter and add to the skillet 1 red onion, finely chopped, 3 tablespoons seasoned flour, ½ teaspoon dried mustard, 1 cup water, and ½ cup fresh lemon juice.

Cook over low heat until the mixture thickens, stirring constantly. Return the skewers to the sauce and cook over low heat for 15 minutes.

Serve with hot buttered noodles dusted with a hefty pinch of nutmeg.

Serves 4

Mushroom Cap
Steak
flour

5

BEEFSTEAK AND ONIONS ON A STICK

Sirloin steak
Pearl onions, large martini type
Peanut oil
Honey
Tarragon vinegar
Ground ginger
Fresh garlic
Green onions

Cut 2 pounds of ¾-inch thick sirloin steak into 1-inch chunks and thread on thin bamboo skewers, alternating each piece of steak with a pearl onion.

Marinate the skewers for 2 hours at room temperature in a mixture consisting of ½ cup oil, 2 tablespoons honey, 3 tablespoons tarragon vinegar, 1 teaspoon ground ginger, 1 clove finely chopped garlic, and ½ cup finely chopped green onions (include the stems).

Broil or barbeque until golden brown on all sides; baste frequently with the marinade.

Serve with hot buttered noodles sprinkled with a dash of nutmeg.

Serves 4

Pearl Onion

Steak

6

SKEWERED BEEFSTEAK L'ORANGE

Steak (sirloin, rib-eye, or lean chuck)
Lemon juice
Salt, pepper
Water chestnuts

Cut a ¾-inch thick steak into 1-inch chunks; dip in lemon juice and sprinkle with salt and pepper.

Alternate the chunks of steak with thin slices of canned water chestnuts on each of 8 butcher skewers.

Broil or barbeque; baste frequently with orange sauce.

ORANGE SAUCE

Vinegar
Sugar
Oranges
Lemon

Simmer 6 tablespoons vinegar with 2 tablespoons sugar until the mixture thickens.

Add the juice of 2 oranges and the juice of 1 lemon with ¼ teaspoon finely slivered orange rind. Simmer for 10 minutes; use hot.

Serves 4

7

SKEWERED STEAK AND KIDNEYS À LA PUB

Lamb kidneys
Steak (sirloin, round, or rib)
Olive oil
Onion
Mushrooms (canned or fresh)
Consommé
Worcestershire sauce
Cornstarch
Dry red wine

Soak 1 pound lamb kidneys in salted cold water for 1 hour; remove membranes and cut kidneys in ¾-inch cubes.

Cut 1 pound of steak in ¾-inch cubes.

Alternate steak and kidney chunks on each of 8 butcher skewers and sauté until brown in 4 tablespoons olive oil.

Add to the skillet 1 chopped onion, 1 cup chopped mushrooms, and ¼ cup consommé; cover and simmer for ¾ of an hour.

Add a mixture of 1 tablespoon Worcestershire sauce, 1 teaspoon cornstarch, and 1 cup dry red wine; cover and simmer for 45 minutes or until tender.

Serve on lightly toasted English muffins and liberally douse with the hot steaming sauce.

Serves 4

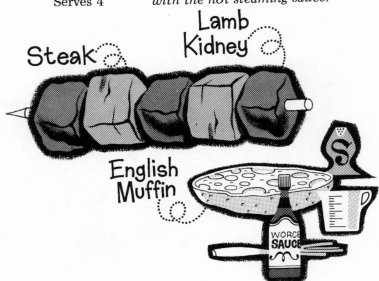

Steak

Lamb
Kidney

English
Muffin

8

STEAK AND OYSTERS BORDEAUX

Oysters (fresh or canned)
White Bordeaux wine
Sirloin steak
One egg
Holland rusk
Butter
Scallions (or green onions)
Green pepper
Celery

Simmer at low heat for 10 minutes 16 oysters in a mixture of their own juice and 1 cup white Bordeaux wine. Save the stock.

Cut a 1-pound, ¾-inch thick sirloin steak into 1-inch squares and alternate steak and cooked oysters on each of four 8-inch bamboo skewers.

Dip skewered oysters and steak into a beaten egg and then roll in bread crumbs made from 3 slices of Holland rusk.

Sauté breaded skewers in 4 tablespoons hot butter until golden brown on all sides.

Add 6 diced scallions (or ½ cup diced green onions), ¼ cup coarsely minced green pepper, and ½ cup diced celery to the skillet; sauté for an additional 10 minutes.

Add the cooking stock and quickly bring to a rolling boil for a minute or so.

Serve with steaming hot rice and cover with spoonfuls of the sauce.

Serves 4

Steak

Oyster

9

BEEFSTEAK DANISH ON A STICK

Steak (sirloin, rib-eye, or lean chuck)
Leaf spinach
Tarragon vinegar
Salt, pepper
Butter
Green onion
Cornstarch
Prepared beef base (or consommé)
Beer
Thyme
Fresh parsley

Cut a 2-pound, ¾-inch thick steak into 1-inch squares and thread on butcher skewers; alternate each piece of steak with several neatly folded leaves of spinach.

Compress the skewered steak on each stick so that the spinach is tightly packed between the chunks of steak.

Brush the steak with a mixture of 2 tablespoons tarragon vinegar, 1 teaspoon salt, and ¼ teaspoon pepper.

Let the skewers stand at room temperature for ½ hour; quickly sauté in very hot butter until brown on all sides.

Add to the skillet a mixture of ½ cup chopped green onions, 1 tablespoon cornstarch, 1 cup prepared beef base (or consommé), ½ cup beer, ¼ teaspoon thyme, and 1 teaspoon finely chopped fresh parsley. Bring to a boil, reduce heat and cook until sauce thickens.

Serve skewers and sauce steaming hot with your favorite recipe for potato pancakes.

Serves 4

Spinach

Steak

10

PEPPERED STEAK ON SKEWERS

Steak (sirloin, rib-eye, or lean chuck)
Pimento, 4-ounce jar
Coarsely ground pepper
Butter
Olive oil
Dry white wine
Light rum

Cut a 2-pound, ¾-inch thick steak and a jar of pimento slices into 1-inch squares; alternate steak and pimento squares on each of 8 butcher skewers.

Spread 2 tablespoons coarsely ground pepper on a piece of waxed paper and lightly dip skewers in the pepper; let stand at room temperature for 1 hour.

Fry quickly in a browned mixture of 2 tablespoons butter and 2 tablespoons olive oil. Remove to a hot platter.

Add to the skillet ⅔ cup dry white wine and 2 tablespoons rum. Bring to a boil and reduce heat. Simmer for 5 minutes while scraping any crust from the bottom of the pan.

Strain the sauce and serve from a gravy boat.

Serves 4

Serve with hot steaming buttered noodles.

11

STEAK ON RYE*

Boned porterhouse steak
Whole fresh mushrooms
Green pepper
Butter
Green onions
Beef consommé
Lemon juice
Rye whiskey
Cornstarch
Salt, pepper, MSG

*Scotch, rum, or bourbon will also do.

Cut 2 pounds of ¾-inch thick steak into 1-inch squares.

Cap 2 dozen mushrooms and parboil the caps for 5 minutes; finely chop the stems and save for the sauce.

Cut 1 green pepper into 1-inch squares and alternate steak, mushroom caps, and green pepper on each of 8 butcher skewers.

Quickly sauté the skewers in 3 tablespoons butter until well browned; remove to a warm platter.

Dice 8 green onions and sauté in the browned butter together with the chopped mushroom stems.

Add to the skillet a mixture of 1 cup beef consommé, the juice of 1 lemon, ½ cup whiskey, ¼ teaspoon salt, ¼ teaspoon pepper, ½ teaspoon MSG, and 1 tablespoon cornstarch; cook with constant stirring for 15 minutes.

Return skewers to the skillet and simmer in the sauce for 10 minutes or until done to taste.

Serve with a liberal dousing of sauce and a garnish of sliced tomatoes and cucumbers.

Serves 4

Steak   Green Pepper

Mushroom Cap

BROCHETTES OF BEEF STROGANOFF

Steak (sirloin or lean chuck)
Prepared white onions, 16-ounce jar
Butter
Cream of mushroom soup, 10½ ounce
    can
Red Burgundy wine
Sour cream

Cut 2 pounds of ¾-inch thick steak into 1-inch squares and thread on each of four 8-inch bamboo skewers, alternating each chunk of steak with a small white onion.

Sauté the skewers until brown on all sides in 4 tablespoons butter.

Add to the skillet 1 can cream of mushroom soup thoroughly mixed with ½ cup red Burgundy wine.

Simmer the skewered steak for 20 minutes. Just before serving stir 2 tablespoons rich sour cream into sauce.

Serves 4

Serve on triangles of toast with a liberal amount of sauce; garnish with fresh parsley.

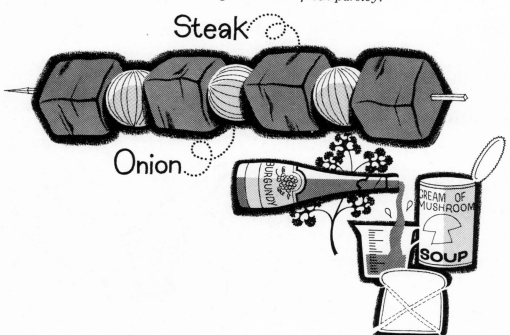

Steak

Onion

13

BROCHETTES OF MEAT AND MIXED VEGETABLES

Steak (sirloin or lean chuck)
Cherry tomatoes
Green pepper
Mushroom caps
Pitted green olives
Olive oil
Prepared barbeque sauce

Cut 1½ pounds of thickly sliced steak into 1-inch squares and thread on each of four 8-inch bamboo skewers, alternating steak with cherry tomatoes, green pepper squares, mushroom caps, and pitted green olives.

Brush with oil and broil or barbeque the skewers until browned on all sides.

Brush with your favorite barbeque sauce just before removing; broil for an additional minute or two on each side.

Serves 4

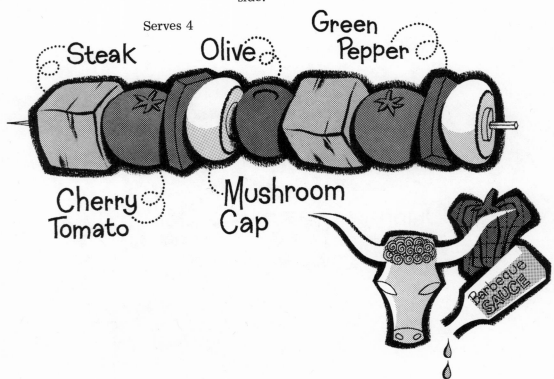

Steak Olive Green Pepper

Cherry Tomato Mushroom Cap

Barbeque SAUCE

14

BEEF TERIYAKI

Steak (sirloin, rib-eye, or lean chuck)
Soy sauce
Dry white wine
Fresh garlic
Sugar
Ground ginger
Mushroom caps, 8-ounce can

Prepare a marinade consisting of ½ cup soy sauce, ¼ cup dry white wine, 1 clove finely chopped fresh garlic, 2 tablespoons sugar, and ½ teaspoon ground ginger.

Cut 1½ pounds of ¾-inch thick steak into 1-inch squares and marinate for 1 hour at room temperature.

Alternate steak and mushroom caps on each of 8 butcher skewers.

Broil or barbeque for 5 minutes on each side or until done to taste; brush frequently with the marinade.

Serves 4

Garnish with fresh parsley and serve with hot steaming rice.

Mushroom Cap

Steak

15

HAWAIIAN MEATBALLS ON A STICK

Lean ground beef
Ground veal
Garlic salt
Salt, pepper
Small white onion
Paprika
Bread crumbs
Honey
Pineapple chunks, 13-ounce can
Ground ginger
Brown sugar
Soy sauce
Prepared chili sauce

Thoroughly mix ¾ pound lean ground beef with ¾ pound ground veal; blend in ⅛ teaspoon garlic salt, ¾ teaspoon salt, ⅛ teaspoon cracked pepper, 3 tablespoons finely minced onion, ½ teaspoon paprika, ½ cup bread crumbs, and ½ cup honey. Shape into 1-inch balls.

Place in a foil-covered broiling pan and broil for 5 minutes, turning once; let cool for 15 minutes.

Carefully alternate cooked meatballs and pineapple chunks on each of four 8-inch bamboo skewers.

Liberally brush with a sauce consisting of ¼ teaspoon ground ginger, ¼ cup brown sugar, ¼ cup soy sauce, and ½ cup chili sauce heated together until sugar dissolves. Return to the pan and broil on all sides until crusty brown.

Serves 4   *Serve with hot steaming rice and a cool rum Bloody Mary.*

16

STEAK AND OYSTERS MONTICELLO

Fresh oysters
Steak (sirloin, rib-eye, or lean chuck)
Butter
Parsley flakes
Fresh cracked pepper
Fresh lemon juice

Poach 18 stewing oysters in their own juice just long enough to bring the liquid to a boil.

Cut a ¾-inch thick steak into 1-inch squares and alternate steak and oysters on each of 8 butcher skewers.

Brush the skewers with 2 tablespoons melted butter; dust with parsley flakes and freshly cracked pepper. Broil or barbeque until browned on all sides.

Sprinkle with fresh lemon juice and serve on triangles of pumpernickel.

Serves 4

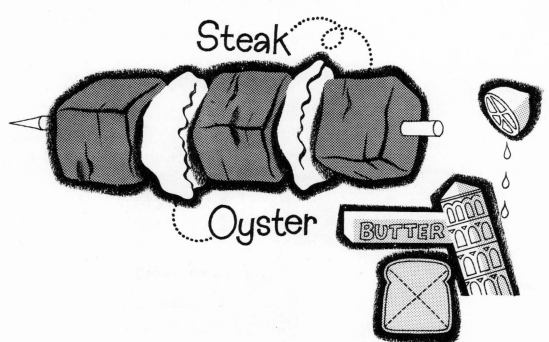

17

STEAK AND LOBSTER EN BROCHETTE

Steak (sirloin, rib-eye, or lean chuck)
Frozen lobster tails
Butter
Lemon juice
Mushroom stems and pieces,
    8-ounce can
Fresh garlic
Salt, pepper
Sauterne
Chopped fresh parsley
Lemon wedges

Cut 2 pounds of 1-inch thick steak into 1-inch cubes.

Cook 2 pounds of lobster tails according to the directions on the package; douse in ice water, remove shells, and cut lobster into 1-inch chunks.

Alternate steak and lobster on each of 8 butcher skewers.

Sauté the skewers in 6 tablespoons hot browned butter for 5 minutes on each side and remove to a heated platter.

Add to the skillet 4 tablespoons lemon juice, an 8-ounce can of drained chopped mushrooms, 1 clove finely chopped garlic, ¼ teaspoon salt, ⅛ teaspoon fresh cracked pepper, ¼ teaspoon MSG, and ½ cup sauterne. Simmer for 5 minutes.

Return the steak and lobster to the skillet and continue to simmer for an additional 15 minutes.

Serve with a liberal dousing of sauce and a garnish of chopped parsley and lemon wedges.

Serves 4

18

EAST INDIAN CURRY—SKEWERED?

Beef steak (sirloin, rib-eye, or lean
    chuck)
Boned lamb steak (rib, loin, or
    shoulder)
Boned veal steak
Green onions
Butter
Ground ginger
Garlic clove
Curry powder
Salt
Dry white wine
Tomatoes

Cut ½ pound beef, ½ pound lamb, and ½ pound veal into
1-inch squares; thread on each of 8 butcher skewers.
Alternate the meats and separate each with a large
green-onion head.

In a skillet lightly toss the finely chopped stems of the green
onions in 4 tablespoons hot browned butter.

Add to the skillet a mixture of ½ teaspoon ground ginger, 1
clove finely chopped garlic, 1 teaspoon curry powder, a
pinch of salt, and 1 cup dry white wine; simmer until the
volume is reduced by one-half.

Add the skewers to the skillet, cover, and slowly cook for
45 minutes.

Just before serving add 2 quartered tomatoes and cook for
5 minutes longer.

Serves 4   *Serve with hot steaming brown rice.*

19

SKEWERED VEAL IN MUSTARD SAUCE

Veal steak
Mushroom caps, 3-ounce jar
Butter
Salt, MSG
Rosemary
Sage
Dry red wine
Dijon mustard
Brown mustard
Paprika
Sour cream
Sweet cream

Cut 2 pounds of ¾-inch thick veal steak into 1-inch squares and thread on each of 8 butcher skewers; alternate each chunk of veal with a mushroom cap.

Prepare a mustard sauce by blending the following: 4 teaspoons Dijon mustard, 4 teaspoons brown mustard, ¼ teaspoon paprika, 1 teaspoon MSG, 2 tablespoons sour cream, and ½ cup sweet cream.

Sauté the skewers in 4 tablespoons hot browned butter until crusty brown on all sides. Season each side with a well-blended mixture of ½ teaspoon each of salt, rosemary, and sage.

Add to the skillet ½ cup dry red wine; simmer for 5 minutes and add the premixed mustard sauce.

Stir and heat until piping hot. (Do not boil.)

Serve on a bed of steaming noodles and douse with the sauce.

Serves 4

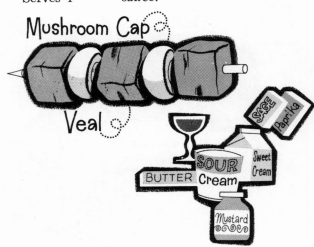

20

BROCHETTES OF VEAL IN MINCEMEAT SAUCE

Veal steak
Mushroom caps, 3-ounce jar
Flour
Butter
White onion (2-inch diameter)
Celery
Prepared mincemeat, 9-ounce package
Dry red wine
Salt, pepper, MSG

Cut 2 pounds of ¾-inch thick veal steak into 1-inch squares and thread on each of four 8-inch bamboo skewers, alternating chunks of veal with mushroom caps.

Dust the skewers with flour and sauté in 6 tablespoons butter until golden brown and crusty on all sides.

Remove the skewers to a warm platter; add to the skillet 1 finely minced onion, 1 cup chopped celery, 1 cup prepared mincemeat, 1 cup dry red wine, ½ teaspoon salt, ¼ teaspoon pepper, and ½ teaspoon MSG; simmer for 15 minutes, stirring frequently.

Return the skewers to the skillet and continue to cook for an additional 15 minutes.

Serve on a bed of hot buttered noodles and cover with the sauce.

Serves 4

Mushroom Cap

Veal

21

SKEWERED VEAL STEAK IN SOUR CREAM

Veal steak (arm or sirloin)
Pitted black olives
Salt, pepper
Bacon
Green onions
Carrot
Fresh garlic clove
Dry red wine
Sour cream
Cornstarch
Water
Lemon juice

Cut a 2-pound, ¾-inch thick veal steak in 1-inch chunks and alternate veal and pitted black olives on each of 8 butcher skewers; rub with salt and pepper.

Fry 6 slices coarsely diced bacon in a large skillet until crisp; drain and discard all but about 1 teaspoon of the fat.

Add to the bacon in the skillet 6 chopped green onions (including stems), 1 thinly sliced carrot, and 1 mashed clove of garlic; toss and sauté the vegetables until golden.

Remove the vegetables from the pan, add skewers and sauté until lightly brown on all sides.

Return the cooked vegetables to the pan together with a mixture of ½ cup dry red wine and ¾ cup sour cream. Cover and slowly cook for ¼ hour. Transfer the skewers to a hot platter.

Make a paste of ½ tablespoon cornstarch, 4 tablespoons water, and 1 tablespoon lemon juice. Blend with liquid in the skillet and cook for a few moments longer to thicken.

Spoon sauce over the skewers and serve with a foil-baked potato.

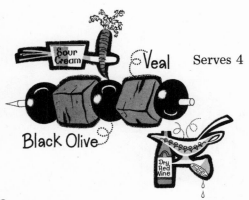

Veal Serves 4

Black Olive

BROCHETTES OF VEAL MAGENTA

Veal steak (arm or sirloin)
Fresh mushrooms, 1 pound
Egg
Milk
Bread crumbs
Grated Parmesan cheese
Butter

Cut 2 pounds of ¾-inch thick veal steak into 1-inch squares; thread on each of 4 bamboo skewers, alternating each piece of veal with a mushroom cap.

Dip the skewers in a batter consisting of 1 egg beaten with 1 tablespoon milk, and bread in a mixture of equal parts fine dry bread crumbs and grated Parmesan cheese.

Sauté skewers in 4 tablespoons browned butter until golden and crisp on all sides.

Serves 4

Serve on squares of garlic toast.

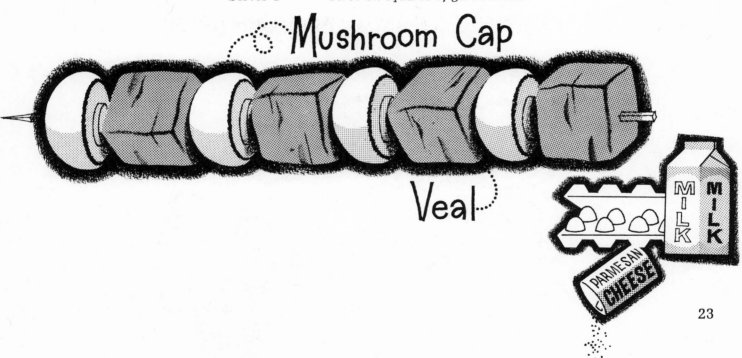

Mushroom Cap

Veal

23

VEAL DANISH ON A SKEWER

Veal steak (arm or shoulder)
Cherry tomatoes
Green pepper
Peanut oil
Fresh garlic clove
Prepared chili sauce
Tarragon vinegar
Pepper

Cut 2 pounds of ¾-inch thick veal steak into 1-inch squares and thread on each of 8 butcher skewers; alternate each piece of veal with a cherry tomato and a green pepper square.

Marinate the skewers for 1 hour in a shallow pan at room temperature in a mixture of ½ cup oil, 1 clove crushed garlic, ¼ cup chili sauce, 2 tablespoons tarragon vinegar, and a dash of freshly cracked pepper. Turn at 15 minute intervals to coat all sides.

Broil or barbeque (turn frequently) until brown on all sides.

Serves 4

Serve with hot buttered carrots and peas.

24

BROCHETTES OF VEAL AND PORK

Veal steak (arm or sirloin)
Lean pork (boned rib or loin chop)
Peanut oil
Onions
Fresh parsley
Green peppers
Tomatoes
Salt, pepper
Fennel seed
Fresh garlic clove

Cut 1 pound each of ¾-inch thick veal and pork into 1-inch squares. Alternate veal and pork on each of 8 butcher skewers; quickly brown in 3–4 tablespoons oil over high heat.

Add to the skillet 2 medium-sized finely chopped onions and 2 tablespoons finely chopped parsley; cook with the brochettes until the onions are transparent. Toss and stir frequently.

Add to the skillet 2 sweet green peppers diced into ½-inch squares, 2 sliced tomatoes, salt and pepper to taste, ½ teaspoon fennel seed, and 1 clove crushed garlic. Cover and cook for 1 hour.

Serve the brochettes on triangles of toast in a bed of the sauce.

Serves 4

Veal

Pork

25

VEAL L'ORANGE EN BROCHETTE

Veal steak (arm or sirloin)
Green pepper
Salt, pepper
Cinnamon
Butter
Spinach
Fresh parsley
Beef bouillon
Orange juice
Cornstarch

Cut 2 pounds of ¾-inch thick veal steak into 1-inch squares and thread on each of 8 butcher skewers; alternate each piece of veal with a 1-inch square of green pepper.

Season the skewers with salt and pepper; dust with cinnamon.

Sauté the skewers in 4 tablespoons browned butter until crusty on all sides; remove the skewers to a heated platter.

Add to the skillet 2 tablespoons butter, 2 cups finely chopped raw spinach, ½ cup chopped parsley, and 1 cup prepared beef bouillon; simmer for 15 minutes.

Return the skewers to the skillet and add a blended mixture of 1 cup orange juice and 1 tablespoon cornstarch; cook for 15 minutes or until the sauce thickens.

Serves 4   *Serve with hot steaming rice.*

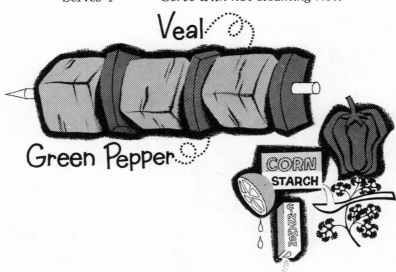

Veal

Green Pepper

CORN STARCH

VEAL MARGUERITE ON A STICK

Veal steak (arm or shoulder)
Sliced potatoes, 16-ounce can
Flour
Olive oil
Shallots (or small green onions)
Fresh garlic clove
Salt
Curry powder
Ruby port

Cut a ¾-inch thick veal steak into 1-inch squares; alternate veal and potato slices on each of 8 butcher skewers.

Dust with flour and sauté in hot olive oil until brown and crusty on all sides. Remove the skewers to a hot platter.

Add to the skillet 8 finely chopped shallots (or green onion bulbs), 1 clove mashed garlic, ⅛ teaspoon salt, 1 teaspoon curry powder, and 3 tablespoons ruby port; simmer the sauce until its volume is reduced by one-half.

Return the skewers to the skillet and cook for about 5 minutes; turn and baste several times with the sauce.

Serves 4   *Serve on toast triangles with hot steaming asparagus.*

Veal Steak

Potato Wafers

flour

27

VEAL KIDNEY KABOBS

Veal kidneys
Salt, pepper
Olive oil
Parsley flakes

Remove fat, membrane, and hard parts from 4 veal kidneys and cut into 1-inch chunks. Soak the pieces in cold water for ½ hour, pat dry, season with salt and pepper, and thread on each of 8 butcher skewers.

Brush with olive oil and sprinkle with parsley flakes.

Align the 8 skewers on a generous portion of aluminum foil, fold, and seal the joints. Bake at 300°F for 1 hour.

Serves 4

Arrange on triangles of toast and serve with broiled bacon and sliced tomatoes.

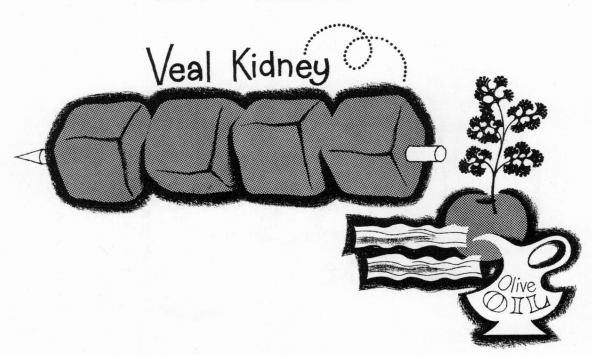

Veal Kidney

Olive OIL

28

SKEWERED VEAL HEART WITH VERMOUTH

Veal hearts
Flour
Butter
Vermouth

Remove the fat from 2 veal hearts; rinse in cold water and pat dry. Cut the hearts into 1-inch chunks and remove veins.

Dust the chunks with flour and thread on each of 8 butcher skewers. Sauté in butter in a large skillet until golden brown.

Add 1 cup of dry vermouth, cover, and simmer for 1 hour.

Serves 4   *Serve with hot buttered noodles.*

Veal Heart

flour

SAUTÉED VEAL EN BROCHETTE

Veal steak (arm or shoulder)
Cherry tomatoes
Mushrooms, 12 whole fresh
Green peppers
Salt, pepper
Paprika
Butter
Green onions
Celery
Fresh garlic clove
Dry red wine
Cornstarch

Cut 2 pounds of ¾-inch thick veal steak into 1-inch squares.

Alternate veal, cherry tomatoes, mushroom caps, and green pepper squares on each of 12 butcher skewers.

Set aside; in a bowl, a mixture of 1 cup diced celery, 6 coarsely chopped green onions with the stems, 1 clove finely minced garlic, and the remaining mushroom pieces.

Season the skewers with salt, pepper, and paprika; sauté in ¼ stick of butter until lightly browned on all sides.

Add the vegetable mixture to the skillet and toss and sauté until the onions are transparent.

Add 1 cup dry red wine mixed with ½ tablespoon cornstarch. Simmer until the sauce thickens.

Serves 4

Serve with a fresh tomato and cucumber salad.

Green Pepper · Cherry Tomato · Veal · Mushroom Cap

SMORGASBORD ON A STICK

Veal steak (arm or shoulder)
Lamb leg steak
Eggplant
Chicken livers, ½ pound
Salt, pepper
Dried basil
Prepared batter mix
Peanut oil
Butter

Cut the following into 1-inch chunks: 1 pound each of ¾-inch thick veal and lamb and ½ medium-sized eggplant, peeled.

Alternate veal, lamb, eggplant, and chicken livers on each of 4 long bamboo skewers.

Season with salt, pepper, and basil.

Dip in a prepared batter and deep fry in hot oil containing 2 tablespoons of butter until golden brown.

Serves 4

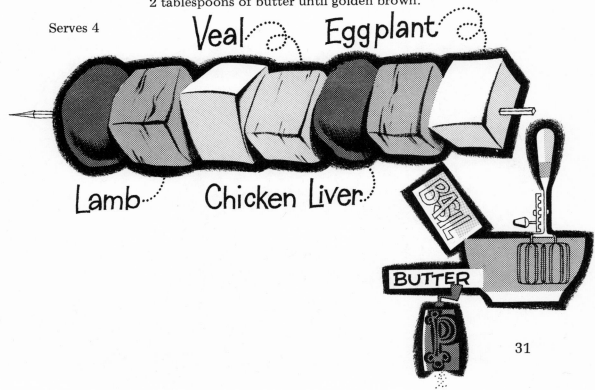

31

BROCHETTES OF LAMB IN CAPER SAUCE

Lamb steak (leg or shoulder)
Pimentoes, 4-ounce jar
Olive oil
White onion, medium-sized
Carrot, medium-sized
Leek
Garlic clove
Salt, pepper
Dry red wine
Butter
Flour
Beef bouillon
Capers

Serves 4

Cut 2 pounds of ¾-inch thick lamb into 1-inch squares and thread on each of 8 butcher skewers; alternate each square of lamb with a pimento square.

Sauté the skewers until brown on all sides in 4 tablespoons hot olive oil.

Add to the skillet 1 coarsely chopped onion, 1 grated carrot, 1 coarsely chopped leek, 1 clove minced garlic, ¼ teaspoon pepper, and 1 cup dry red wine; cover and simmer for 30 minutes.

In a sauce pan combine 4 tablespoons butter, 1 tablespoon flour mixed with 1 cup beef bouillon, and 4 tablespoons capers. Simmer for 10 minutes.

Bed the skewers in hot steaming rice covered with the sauce.

Pimento

Lamb

32

LAMB DANISH ON A STICK

Lamb steak (arm or shoulder)
Mushroom caps, 3-ounce jar
Butter
Salt, pepper
White onion, medium-sized
Buttermilk

Cut 2 pounds of ¾-inch thick lamb into 1-inch squares; alternate lamb and mushroom caps on each of 8 butcher skewers; season with salt and pepper; brown the skewers in 4 tablespoons melted butter.

Add to the skillet 1 finely chopped onion and 1 cup buttermilk; cook slowly for 20 minutes; turn the skewers from time to time and baste with the sauce.

Serves 4

Serve with hot buttered noodles and smother with the sauce.

Mushroom Cap

Lamb

P S

Buttermilk

33

SKEWERED LAMB CANTONESE

Lean ground lamb
Salt, pepper, MSG
Mushroom caps, 3-ounce jar
Bamboo shoots, 6-ounce can
Egg
Instant flour
Peanut oil
Chicken bouillon
Green peppers
Pineapple slices, 15-ounce can
Cornstarch
Soy sauce
Sugar
Vinegar
Pineapple juice

Blend ⅛ teaspoon salt and ⅛ teaspoon pepper with 1½ pounds ground lamb. Form 1-inch balls and carefully thread on each of 4 long bamboo skewers; alternate each lamb ball with a mushroom cap and a ¼-inch slice of bamboo shoot.

Prepare a batter by mixing 1 egg and 3 tablespoons water with ½ cup flour. Brush or spoon the batter onto the skewers; deep fry until golden brown in hot oil.

Remove the skewers to a warmed platter.

In a skillet add ½ cup chicken bouillon, 2 green peppers cut in ½-inch squares, and pineapple slices cut into 6 wedges each; simmer for 10 minutes.

Blend 1 tablespoon cornstarch, 1 tablespoon soy sauce, ½ cup sugar, ½ teaspoon MSG, ½ cup vinegar, and ½ cup pineapple juice and add to the skillet; stir until the sauce thickens.

Place the skewered lamb in the skillet and simmer for 10 minutes.

Serves 4   *Serve with hot steaming rice.*

Ground Lamb

Mushroom Cap   Bamboo Shoot

34

SKEWERED LAMB IN PINEAPPLE SAUCE

Lean ground lamb
Egg
Bread crumbs
Fresh pineapple
Cinnamon
Salt, pepper
Paprika
White onion, medium-sized
Butter
Lemon juice
Sugar
Sherry

Serves 4

Add 1 beaten egg and 2 tablespoons bread crumbs to 1½ pounds lean ground lamb; blend thoroughly.

Form mixture into 1-inch balls and thread on skewers; alternate each lamb ball with 1-inch cubes of fresh pineapple.

Dust with cinnamon, paprika, salt, and pepper and broil over low heat until brown and crispy on all sides.

In a skillet sauté 1 finely chopped onion in 3 tablespoons butter until transparent; stir in a mixture of 1 tablespoon lemon juice, ¼ cup sugar, and ½ cup sherry. Simmer for 10 minutes.

Serve the skewered lamb on triangles of toast and garnish with steaming rice smothered with the prepared sauce.

Ground Lamb

Pineapple

BROCHETTES OF LAMB MADELEINE

Lamb steak (arm or shoulder)
Dried figs
Rosé wine
Fresh cracked pepper
Bay leaf
Oregano
Paprika
Olive oil

Cut 2 pounds of ¾-inch thick lamb slices into 1-inch chunks.

Alternate lamb and figs on each of 4 long bamboo skewers.

Cover the skewers in a shallow pan with a mixture of 3 cups rosé wine, ¼ teaspoon fresh cracked pepper, ½ of a crumpled bay leaf, ⅛ teaspoon oregano, and ¼ teaspoon paprika; marinate in the refrigerator for 4 hours.

Remove, pat dry, and brush with olive oil. Barbeque or broil at moderate heat until the lamb is well browned on all sides.

Serve with hot steaming rice cooked with a tablespoon of white raisins per serving.

Serves 4

36

SKEWERS OF PERSIAN LAMB

Lamb steak (arm or shoulder)
Olive oil
White wine
Lemon juice
Onion, medium-sized
Tarragon
Chick peas, 15-ounce can
Salt, pepper
Sesame seed
Paprika

Cut 2 pounds of thickly cut lamb steak into 1-inch squares.

Marinate the lamb for 1 hour at room temperature in a mixture of ½ cup olive oil, 1 cup white wine, 2 tablespoons lemon juice, 1 diced onion, and a pinch of tarragon.

Thread the lamb on each of four 10-inch thin bamboo skewers; alternate each piece of lamb with a chick pea.

Pat dry and brush with olive oil; dust with salt, pepper, ground sesame seed, and paprika.

Broil or barbeque until crispy brown on all sides.

Serves 4

Serve with hot steaming saffron rice.

Lamb

Chick Pea

LAMB AND CHICKEN LIVERS ON A STICK

Lamb steak (arm or shoulder)
Chicken livers, 1 pound
Butter

Cut 1½ pounds of ¾-inch thick lamb into 1-inch squares; alternate lamb and chicken livers on each of 8 butcher skewers.

Brush with melted butter and broil or barbeque until crispy brown.

Serves 4

Serve with hot steaming noodles and a garnish of parsley.

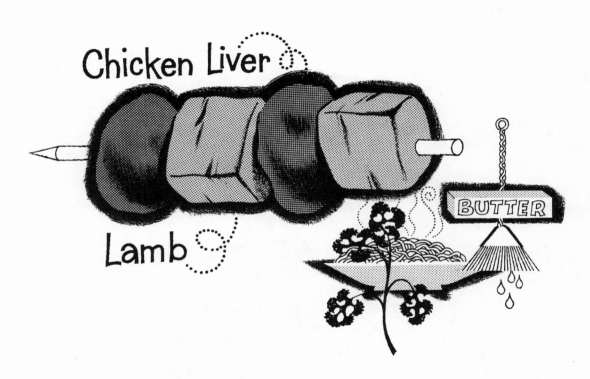

38

MUK-LOU-BEH (BROCHETTES OF LAMB AND EGGPLANT)

Lamb steak (arm, shoulder or leg)
Eggplant
Butter
Dry white wine
Powdered saffron
Ground allspice
Salt, pepper

Cut 1½ pounds of thickly sliced lamb and 1 large peeled eggplant into 1-inch chunks. Alternate lamb and eggplant on each of four 10-inch bamboo skewers.

Sauté in hot butter until brown on all sides; remove to a warm platter.

Add to the skillet a mixture of 2 cups dry white wine and ⅛ teaspoon of each of the following: saffron, allspice, salt, and pepper. Simmer the ingredients for 5 minutes; scrape any crust from the pan and blend with the broth.

Return the skewers to the skillet, cover, and simmer for 20 minutes.

Serves 4   *Serve with hot steaming kasha (buckwheat groats).*

SKEWERED LAMB WITH MUSHROOMS

Lamb (arm, shoulder, or leg)
Mushroom caps, 3-ounce jar
Olive oil
Dry white wine
Lemon juice
Onion
Salt, pepper

Cut 2 pounds of thickly sliced lamb into 1-inch squares; marinate overnight in the refrigerator in a mixture of ½ cup olive oil, 1 cup dry white wine, 4 tablespoons lemon juice, 1 medium onion, diced, a pinch of salt, and a twist of fresh cracked pepper.

Pat dry and thread the lamb on each of four 10-inch bamboo skewers; alternate each piece of lamb with a mushroom cap.

Broil or barbeque until brown on all sides.

Serves 4   *Serve with hot steaming rice and a garnish of watercress.*

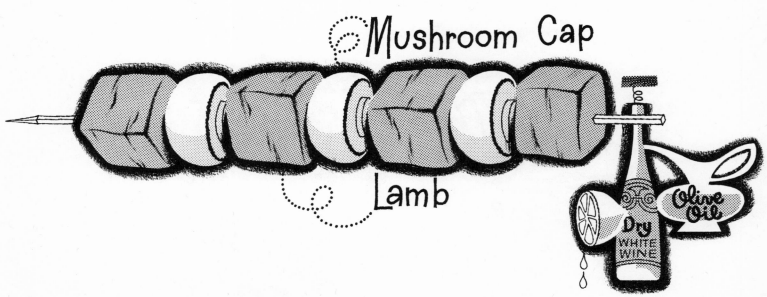

SKEWERED LAMB WITH MINT SAUCE

Lamb steak (arm or shoulder)
Pimento, 4-ounce jar
Wine vinegar
Dried mint
Fresh garlic clove
Olive oil
Salt, pepper, MSG

Cut 2 pounds of ½-inch thick lamb into 1-inch squares. Alternate lamb and 1-inch squares of pimento on each of 8 butcher skewers.

Marinate the skewers for 1 hour at room temperature in a mixture of 2 cups wine vinegar, ½ teaspoon dried mint, and 1 mashed garlic clove.

Remove and pat dry; brush with olive oil; sprinkle with salt, pepper, and MSG; broil or barbeque until crispy brown on all sides. Baste occasionally with the marinade.

Serves 4   *Serve with hot steaming buckwheat groats.*

41

SKEWERED LAMB WITH SAUTÉED CELERY

Lamb steak (arm, shoulder, or leg)
Mushroom caps, 3-ounce jar
Celery stalks
Olive oil
Dry sherry
Dried mint
Salt

Cut 2 pounds of thickly sliced lamb into 1-inch squares and alternate lamb and mushroom caps on each of 8 butcher skewers.

Slice 3 celery stalks into ¼-inch pieces and sauté in ¼ cup olive oil for 15 minutes; scoop into a warm bowl.

Sauté the lamb and mushrooms at high heat in remaining oil for 5 minutes on each side.

Add to the skillet a mixture of ½ cup dry sherry, ¼ teaspoon dried mint, and ¼ teaspoon salt; simmer uncovered for 10 minutes.

Return the celery to the skillet and continue to simmer for an additional 10 minutes.

Serves 4

Serve with a garnish of hot buttered mixed garden vegetables.

Mushroom Cap

Lamb

42

SKEWERED LAMB HEART FLAMBÉ

Lamb hearts
Salt, pepper
Mushrooms, 24 whole fresh
Butter
Green pepper
Dijon-style mustard
Lemon juice
Paprika
Dried tarragon
Beef bouillon
Cognac

Cook 2 lamb hearts for 30 minutes in salted water. Cool and then cut the hearts into 1-inch chunks; remove veins.

Sprinkle the pieces with salt and pepper and thread on each of 8 butcher skewers, alternating each chunk of meat with a large mushroom cap.

Sauté the skewers in ½ stick of hot butter until well browned on all sides; remove to a hot platter.

Add to the skillet the remaining finely chopped mushroom stems, 1 small diced green pepper, 2 tablespoons Dijon-style mustard, the juice of ½ lemon, ½ teaspoon paprika, a sprinkle of tarragon, ½ cup beef bouillon, and 2 ounces Cognac. Cook the mixture over low heat for 10 minutes; stir frequently.

Return the skewers to the skillet and continue to cook for 20 minutes.

Carefully warm ¼ cup Cognac in a small sauce pan, ignite, and pour over the skewers.

Serves 4   *Serve with hot buttered noodles.*

Mushroom Cap

Lamb Heart

Butter

43

SKEWERED HAM PARMESAN

Cooked ham
Cherry tomatoes
Worcestershire sauce
Olive oil
Bread crumbs
Parmesan cheese

Cut 1½ pounds of ¾-inch thick slices of cooked ham into 1-inch squares and thread onto each of 8 butcher skewers; alternate each chunk of ham with a cherry tomato.

Brush each skewer with a mixture of 1 tablespoon Worcestershire sauce and 1 tablespoon olive oil; bread with a mixture of ⅓ cup fine dry bread crumbs and ⅓ cup Parmesan cheese.

Bake in the oven at 300° F. for about 30 minutes or until crumbs are golden brown.

Serve with fresh pineapple slices sprinkled with brown sugar.

Serves 4

Cherry Tomato

Ham

44

GRECIAN HAM EN BROCHETTE

Ham steak
Large white seedless grapes
Butter
Brown sugar
Dry red wine
Ground ginger

Cut 1½ pounds of ¾-inch thick slices of ham into 1-inch squares.

Alternate ham and grapes on each of 8 butcher skewers.

Melt ½ stick butter in the skillet over low heat; stir in 1 tablespoon brown sugar.

Sauté the skewered ham and grapes until well browned on all sides.

Add 1 cup dry red wine to the skillet and lightly sprinkle the skewers with ginger; cook for 10 minutes.

Serve with steaming rice or mixed with a generous quantity of dry roasted cashew nuts.

Serves 4

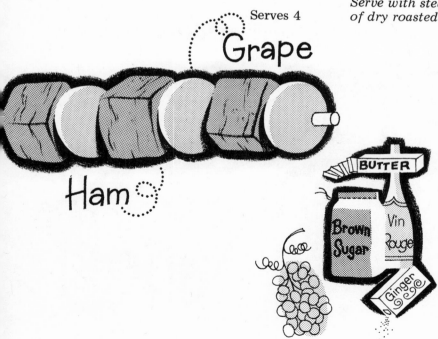

Grape

Ham

45

SKEWERED HAM AND APRICOTS

Dried apricots
Cooked ham
Ground cloves
Sherry
Pineapple preserves

Soak ½ cup dried apricots in 1 cup sherry for 1 hour; pat dry and save the sherry.

Cut 1½ pounds of ¾-inch thick slices of cooked ham into 1-inch squares.

Alternate ham and marinated apricots on each of 8 butcher skewers.

Arrange in a shallow baking pan, dust with cloves, and cover with ¼ cup pineapple preserves mixed with the reserved sherry.

Bake in a moderate oven 350° for 35 minutes or until browned. Turn and baste often.

Serves 4

Serve with baked sweet potatoes.

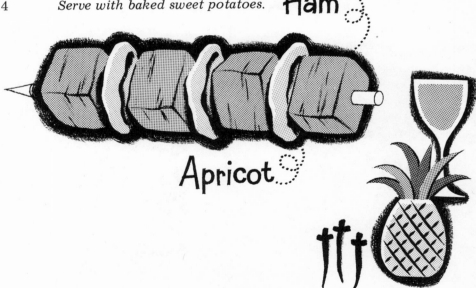

Ham

Apricot

46

SKEWERED HAM HAWAIIAN

Cooked ham
Canned pineapple slices
Stuffed green olives
Butter
Pepper
Paprika

Cut 2 pounds of ½-inch thick slices of cooked ham into 1-inch chunks and cut 6 pineapple slices into 1-inch squares.

Alternate ham, pineapple, and olives on each of four 8-inch bamboo skewers.

Brush with melted butter, season with freshly cracked pepper and paprika; broil 5 minutes on each side.

Serves 4

Douse with raisin sauce and serve with hot steaming rice.

RAISIN SAUCE

Brown sugar
Cornstarch
Mustard powder
Cloves
Allspice
Cinnamon
Wine vinegar
Seedless raisins
Butter
Water

Combine 1 cup brown sugar, 1 tablespoon cornstarch, a dash of mustard powder, ⅛ teaspoon ground cloves, ¼ teaspoon ground allspice, and ¼ teaspoon cinnamon in the top of a double boiler.

Mix ½ cup wine vinegar and 2 cups water and add to the dry mixture.

Stir and cook until the sauce comes to a boil and is thick and smooth; add 1 cup seedless raisins and continue to cook over boiling water for 30 minutes. Stir in 2 tablespoons butter and serve.

Ham   Olive

Pineapple

Raisin
Sauce

BROCHETTES OF BROILED PORK

Pork tenderloin
Soy sauce
Salt, pepper
Ground ginger
Brown sugar
Cherry tomatoes

Cut 2 pounds of pork tenderloin into 1-inch cubes.

Marinate in the refrigerator for 2 hours in a mixture of 1 cup soy sauce, dash of salt, ½ teaspoon pepper, ¼ teaspoon ginger, and 1 teaspoon brown sugar.

Thread the pieces of pork onto each of 4 long bamboo skewers; alternate each piece of pork with a small cherry tomato.

Brush with the marinade and broil or barbeque until thoroughly cooked.

Serves 4

Serve with sautéed banana halves well browned in butter.

Cherry Tomato

Pork Steak

BROCHETTES OF BRAISED PORK IN BURGUNDY SAUCE

Pork tenderloin
Eggplant, medium-sized
Peanut oil
White Burgundy
Butter
Brown sugar
Green onions
Lemon slices
Cornstarch

Cut 2 pounds of pork tenderloin into 1-inch cubes; thread on each of 8 butcher skewers, alternating each piece of pork with a cube of peeled eggplant. Quickly brown on all sides in 1 tablespoon oil.

Remove the skewers from the pan and add to the skillet 1 cup white Burgundy, 2 tablespoons butter, 2 tablespoons brown sugar, 6 finely chopped green onions (heads and stems), and 4 thin lemon slices; bring to a boil.

Return the skewers to the skillet; cover and simmer for about 1 hour or until tender.

Remove the skewers to a warm platter; add 1 teaspoon cornstarch mixed with a little cold water to thicken the sauce.

Spoon sauce over the skewers and serve with a garnish of whole, tart cranberries.

Pork Steak

Serves 4

Eggplant

BROWN SUGAR WHITE BURGUN Cranberry

49

SPICY PORK ON SKEWERS

Pork tenderloin
Green pepper
Mushroom caps, 3-ounce jar
Peanut oil
Tarragon vinegar
Fresh garlic
Prepared chili sauce
Chili powder
Brown sugar
Salt

Cut 2 pounds of pork tenderloin into 1-inch cubes; thread cubes on each of 8 butcher skewers, alternating each piece of pork with a square of green pepper and a mushroom cap.

Prepare a marinade consisting of ⅓ cup oil, 1 cup tarragon vinegar, 1 clove finely chopped garlic, ⅓ cup chili sauce, ¼ teaspoon chili powder, ¼ cup brown sugar, and ½ teaspoon salt. Marinate the skewered pork in the refrigerator for 2 hours.

Broil or barbeque the skewers under moderate heat until brown and thoroughly cooked; baste occasionally with the sauce.

Serve with hot buttered noodles and a garnish of steaming asparagus tips.

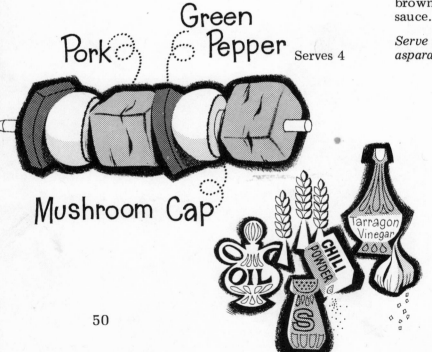

Pork

Green Pepper   Serves 4

Mushroom Cap

50

KUMQUAT MAE

Pork tenderloin
Preserved kumquats, 20-ounce can
Flour
Olive oil
Bamboo shoots, 6-ounce can
Green onions
Mushroom stems and pieces,
    8-ounce can
Garlic
Beef bouillon
Soy sauce
Ginger
Pepper, MSG
Sweet peas, 8-ounce can

Cut 2 pounds of pork tenderloin into 1-inch chunks; arrange on each of 8 butcher skewers, alternating each piece of pork with a kumquat.

Dust lightly with flour and sauté in ½ cup hot olive oil until cooked through and brown and crusty on all sides; remove the skewers.

Add to the skillet thinly sliced bamboo shoots, 6 coarsely chopped green onions and stems, mushroom stems and pieces (drained), and 1 mashed garlic clove; sauté for 15 minutes.

Add to the skillet a mixture of 1 cup beef bouillon, ¼ cup soy sauce, ¼ teaspoon ginger, ½ teaspoon MSG, and a dash of pepper; bring to a slow boil. Return the skewers to the skillet and simmer for 30 minutes.

Add drained sweet green peas to the skillet 5 minutes before serving.

Serves 4   *Serve with hot steaming rice.*

Kumquat

Pork

51

SKEWERED BARBEQUE PORK WITH RUM SAUCE

Pork tenderloin
Anchovy-stuffed olives
Dark rum
Soy sauce
Brown sugar

Cut 2 pounds of pork tenderloin into 1-inch cubes.

Thread pork chunks on each of 4 long bamboo skewers; alternate each piece of pork with an anchovy-stuffed olive.

Brush with a mixture of 3 tablespoons dark rum, 3 tablespoons soy sauce, and 3 tablespoons brown sugar.

Broil or barbeque slowly until the meat is well browned and cooked through.

Serves 4   *Serve with hot steaming rice cooked with diced green pepper.*

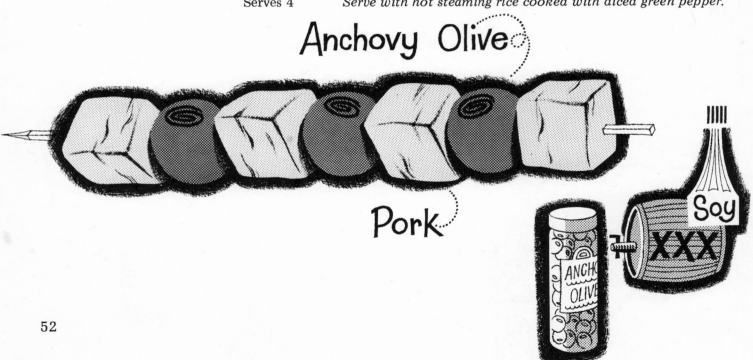

Anchovy Olive

Pork

Soy

52

BARBEQUED CHINESE PORK ON SKEWERS

Pork tenderloin
Soy sauce
Dry mustard
Fresh garlic
Celery seed
Ground ginger
Dry white wine
MSG
Pitted black olives

Cut 2 pounds of pork tenderloin into 1-inch cubes and marinate in a mixture of 1 cup soy sauce, ½ teaspoon dry mustard, 1 mashed garlic clove, ½ teaspoon celery seed, ½ teaspoon ginger, ½ cup dry white wine, and ½ teaspoon MSG.

Alternate pork and pitted black olives on each of 8 butcher skewers.

Broil or barbeque until cooked through and crispy brown, basting frequently with the marinade.

Serves 4

Serve with hot steaming rice cooked with 1 tablespoon white raisins per serving.

Pork

Black Olive

53

CASHEW PORK ON A STICK

Dry roasted cashews
Soy sauce
Onion powder
Celery seed
MSG
Fresh garlic
Tabasco sauce
Lean pork
Fresh sweet red peppers
Olive oil

In a blender or mortar, make a soft paste by combining ½ cup dry roasted cashews, 2 tablespoons soy sauce, ½ teaspoon onion powder, ½ teaspoon celery seed, ½ teaspoon MSG, 1 small garlic clove, and 4 drops Tabasco sauce.

Cut 2 pounds of lean pork into 1-inch cubes and rub the paste into the cubes.

Cut 2 sweet red peppers (or canned pimentoes if not available) into 1-inch squares and alternate pork and peppers on 4 long, thin bamboo skewers.

Brush lightly with olive oil and broil or barbeque slowly until cooked through and crusty brown on all sides.

Serves 4

Serve on hot steaming rice with a hot applesauce garnish.

GLAZED PORK EN BROCHETTE

Pork tenderloin
Pitted green olives
Cherry tomatoes
Tomato sauce
Cognac
Honey
Wine vinegar
Green onions
Fresh garlic
Worcestershire sauce
Tabasco sauce

Cut 2 pounds of pork tenderloin into 1-inch cubes.

Alternate pork, pitted green olives, and cherry tomatoes on each of 4 thin bamboo skewers.

Prepare a basting sauce consisting of 1 cup tomato sauce, 2 tablespoons Cognac, ¼ cup honey, 1 tablespoon wine vinegar, ½ cup finely chopped green onions (heads and stems), 1 mashed garlic clove, ½ teaspoon Worcestershire sauce, and 3 drops Tabasco sauce.

Broil or barbeque until cooked through and well browned on all sides; baste frequently with the sauce.

Serves 4   *Serve with hot steaming brown rice.*

Cherry Tomato

Pork   Olive

55

SKEWERED PORK CANTONESE

Pork tenderloin
Green pepper
Water chestnuts, 8-ounce can
Chicken bouillon
Honey
Cognac
Lemon juice
Fresh garlic
Ginger
Cinnamon
MSG
Olive oil

Cut 2 pounds of pork tenderloin, 2 green peppers, and water chestnuts into 1-inch chunks; alternate pork, green pepper, and water chestnuts on each of 4 thin bamboo skewers.

Combine 1 cup chicken bouillon, ¼ cup soy sauce, ¼ cup honey, 1 tablespoon Cognac, 1 tablespoon lemon juice, 1 mashed garlic clove, ¼ teaspoon ginger, 1 teaspoon cinnamon, and 1 teaspoon MSG; marinate the skewered meat and vegetables in a shallow pan for 1 hour at room temperature.

Brush with olive oil and broil or barbeque at low heat until cooked through and crispy brown; baste frequently with the marinade.

Serves 4

Serve with hot steaming buckwheat groats.

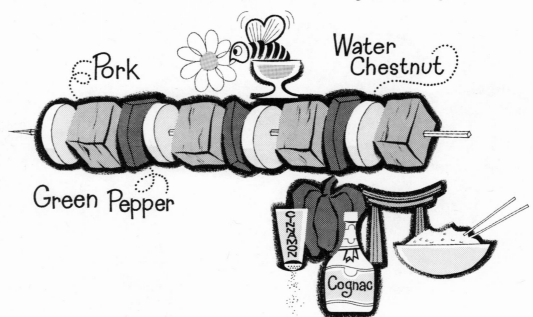

Pork

Water Chestnut

Green Pepper

CINAMON

Cognac

HONG KONG PORK ON A STICK

Pork tenderloin
Dry red wine
Soy sauce
Peanut oil
Pumpkin pie spice
Dry mustard
Pepper, MSG
Brown sugar
Pimento, 4-ounce jar

Cut 2 pounds of pork tenderloin into 1-inch cubes; marinate in a shallow pan for 1 hour at room temperature in a mixture of 1 cup dry red wine, 2 tablespoons soy sauce, 2 tablespoons oil, ½ teaspoon pumpkin pie spice, ½ teaspoon dry mustard, ¼ teaspoon pepper, ½ teaspoon MSG, and 1 teaspoon brown sugar.

Alternate pork and pimento squares on each of 8 butcher skewers; broil slowly on each side until cooked through and crispy brown; baste frequently with the marinade.

Serve on a bed of hot steaming rice and garnish with thinly sliced tomatoes sprinkled with lime juice.

Serves 4

Pimento

Pork Steak

SOY

Dry RED WINE

BEEF, BEER, AND BACON

Steak (sirloin, rib, or chuck)
Bacon (thickly sliced)
Peanut oil
White onions, 2 medium-sized
Beer
Dijon mustard
Sugar
Black pepper

Cut 2 pounds of ¾-inch thick steak into 1-inch squares; thread steak on each of 4 bamboo skewers, alternating each piece of beef with a 1-inch square of bacon.

Brown the skewers in oil along with sliced onions; remove the skewers.

Add to the skillet a mixture of 1 can of beer, 2 teaspoons Dijon mustard, 1 teaspoon sugar, and ¼ teaspoon black pepper; simmer slowly for 10 minutes.

Return the skewers to the skillet and continue to simmer for 30 minutes.

Serves 4   *Serve with a generous portion of potato chips.*

Beef Steak

Bacon

PEPPERED BACON ON SKEWERS

Canadian bacon
Small whole potatoes, 16-ounce can
Olive oil
Salt
Coarsely ground pepper
Paprika
Rye toast

Cut a 2-pound piece of Canadian bacon into 1-inch chunks and thread on each of 4 long bamboo skewers, alternating the bacon chunks with small whole potatoes.

Brush with a generous quantity of olive oil; season with salt, coarsely ground pepper, and paprika; broil or barbeque on all sides until golden brown.

Dust lightly with ground cinnamon.

Serve on triangles of toast and accompany with a fresh garden salad.

Serves 4

Canadian Bacon

Potato

BROCHETTES OF RABBIT IN SPINACH SAUCE

Rabbit
Green pepper
Sauterne
Leaf spinach (fresh or frozen)
Fresh parsley sprigs
Green onions
Dried basil
Butter
Flour

Bone a 3-pound rabbit retaining as many large pieces of meat as possible; cut the meat into bite-size chunks.

Alternate meat and green pepper squares on each of 4 long bamboo skewers.

Simmer in a skillet in 3 cups sauterne for 20 minutes; remove the skewers.

Add to the skillet ½ pound leaf spinach, ¼ cup parsley sprigs, the diced heads and stems of 6 green onions, and 1 teaspoon basil; simmer for 10 minutes.

Add 3 tablespoons butter and 2 tablespoons flour to the cooked greens and blend the entire contents of the skillet in a blender.

Return the sauce and the skewered rabbit to the skillet and simmer for 15 minutes.

Serve with a fresh garden salad.

Green Pepper

Serves 4

Rabbit

SALAMI STUCK ON A STICK

Soft kosher salami (unsliced)
Brussel sprouts (frozen)
Olive oil

Cut 1½ pounds of soft kosher salami into 1-inch chunks; thread on each of 4 bamboo skewers, alternating each piece of salami with a thawed but uncooked brussel sprout.

Brush the skewers with olive oil and broil or barbeque for 5 minutes on each side or until nicely browned.

Serve on triangles of garlic toast with a garnish of pickle relish. Wash down with your favorite brand of red pop.

Serves 4

Brussel Sprout

Salami

Pickle Relish

OLIVE OIL

61

HOT DAWGS IN SHERRY

All-beef frankfurters
Anchovy-stuffed olives
Steak sauce
Fresh lemon juice
Worcestershire sauce
Dry sherry
Instant flour
Water

Cut 8 frankfurters into 1-inch lengths; thread frankfurter segments alternately with anchovy-stuffed olives on each of 8 butcher skewers.

Broil or barbeque the skewers until the frankfurters are crispy brown on all sides.

In a sauce pan combine one cup steak sauce, 4 tablespoons fresh lemon juice, 2 tablespoons Worcestershire sauce, and ¼ cup dry sherry; heat but do not boil.

Blend 1 tablespoon instant flour with a little cold water and add to the sauce. Stir over low heat until thickened.

Serves 4

Arrange the skewers on triangles of toast and douse with the heated sauce.

Anchovy Stuffed Olive

Frankfurter

FLOUR INSTANT

Steak Sauce

62

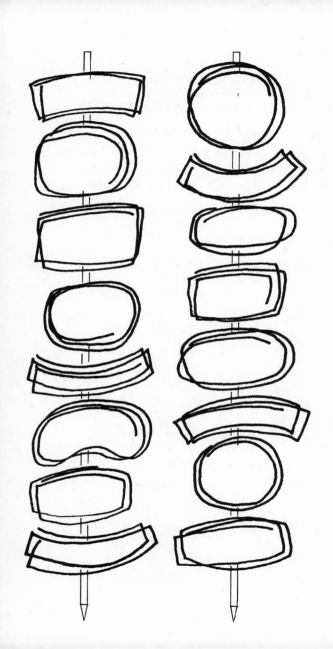

POULTRY

BROCHETTES OF SWEET AND SOUR CHICKEN

Chicken breasts
Flour
Salt
Peanut oil
Garlic cloves
Pineapple chunks, 13-ounce can
Sweet pickles, 8-ounce jar
Soy sauce
Green pepper
Cornstarch
Tomato

Carefully bone 3 large chicken breasts; cut the meat into 1-inch chunks and thread on each of 8 butcher skewers.

Coat the skewers with a mixture of 1 cup flour and ½ teaspoon salt.

Sauté 2 cloves finely minced garlic in ½ cup hot oil; sauté the skewered chicken until golden brown on all sides.

Add to the skillet a mixture of the juice from a can of pineapple chunks, the liquid from a jar of sweet pickles, and 2 tablespoons soy sauce; bring to a boil.

Add pineapple chunks, diced pickles, and 1 green pepper cut into strips. Thicken with a mixture of 1 tablespoon cornstarch and a little cold water; add a large tomato cut into wedges.

Serve with hot steaming rice.

Chicken

Serves 4

64

CHICKEN CURRY EN BROCHETTE

Chicken breasts
Pitted black olives
Butter
Paprika
Chicken base (or bouillon)
Curry powder
Dry white wine
Mushroom stems and pieces,
    4-ounce can
Shredded coconut
Cooked crumpled bacon
Cornstarch

Carefully remove the meat from 3 chicken breasts; retain as many large pieces as possible.

Cut the chicken into 1-inch cubes and alternate chicken and pitted black olives on each of four 8-inch bamboo skewers.

Sauté the skewers until golden brown in a mixture of ¼ stick butter and ¼ teaspoon paprika. Remove to a warm platter.

Add to the skillet a mixture consisting of 1 cup prepared chicken base (or chicken bouillon), 1 teaspoon curry powder, ½ cup dry white wine, 1 tablespoon cornstarch, and ¼ cup shredded coconut. Drain a 4-ounce can of mushroom stems and pieces; add to the mixture.

Cook for 15 minutes; stir frequently.

Return the skewers to the skillet and cook until piping hot.

Dust with ½ cup bacon crumbs and serve over hot steamed rice.

Serves 4

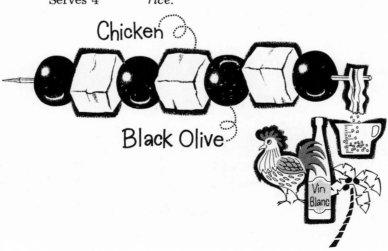

Chicken

Black Olive

Vin Blanc

BROCHETTES OF CHICKEN AND VEAL PILAFF

Chicken breast
Veal (arm or sirloin)
Butter
White onion, medium-sized
Chicken bouillon
Oregano
Salt, pepper, MSG
Tomato paste
Raisins, seedless

Skin and bone 2 large chicken breasts and cut into cubes; thread on butcher skewers, alternating each piece of chicken with a 1-inch square of veal steak cut from 1 pound of ¾-inch thick slices.

Sauté the skewers in ½ stick butter together with 1 finely chopped onion; brown on all sides.

Add 1 can of chicken bouillon, 1 teaspoon oregano, ½ teaspoon MSG, and salt and pepper.

Simmer for 20 minutes; stir occasionally.

Add 1 teaspoon tomato paste and ½ cup seedless raisins. Cook for an additional 10 minutes.

Serve with steaming brown rice.

Serves 4

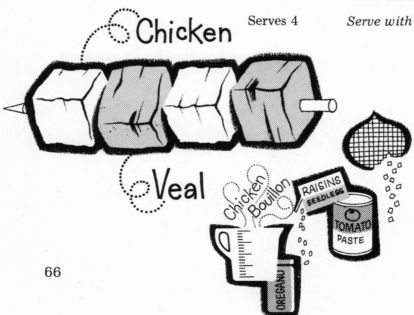

66

CHICKEN KIEV EN BROCHETTE

Fresh garlic
Chicken breast
Parsley
Flour
Egg
Bread crumbs
Butter

Run 8 butcher skewers through a large garlic clove.

Carefully remove the skin and bones from 2 large chicken breasts; retain the meat in one or two solid pieces.

Cut the chicken into 1-inch chunks and thread tightly on each skewer. Between each piece of chicken place a sprig of fresh parsley.

Dust the skewers with flour, dip in a beaten egg, and roll in bread crumbs.

Sauté in ¼ stick of butter until golden brown on all sides.

Garnish with watercress and serve with hot buttered string beans.

Serves 4

67

SWEET BARBEQUE DUCK ON SKEWERS

Duckling (fresh or frozen)
Sweet black cherries, 16-ounce can
MSG, pepper
Ginger
Smoked salt
Honey
Butter

Skin and bone a 3-pound duckling; discard the fat and retain the meat in as many large pieces as possible. Cut into 1-inch chunks.

Alternate chunks of duck and black cherries on each of 4 long bamboo skewers.

Dust with a mixture of ¼ teaspoon each of MSG, pepper, ginger, and smoked salt. Broil or barbeque the skewers under low to medium heat.

When golden brown, baste with a mixture of ⅓ cup honey and 2 tablespoons melted butter; continue to broil for about 10 minutes; turn and baste frequently.

Serve with saffron rice and a garnish of lemon wedges and a sprig of parsley.

Serves 4

Duck

Black Cherry

BUTTER

68

SKEWERED DUCK WITH PINEAPPLE AND BRANDY

Duck (fresh or frozen)
Water chestnuts, 8-ounce can
Peanut oil
Flour
White onion, medium-sized
Crushed pineapple, 13-ounce can
Raisins
Dark brown sugar
Brandy

Skin and bone a 3-pound duckling; discard the fat and retain as many large pieces of meat as possible.

Alternate 1-inch chunks of the meat with $\frac{1}{8}$-inch thick slices of water chestnuts on each of 4 long bamboo skewers.

Roll the skewers in flour and sauté in $\frac{1}{4}$ cup hot oil until brown on all sides.

Add to the skillet a mixture of 1 finely chopped onion, 1 can crushed pineapple with its syrup, 3 tablespoons raisins, and 2 tablespoons dark brown sugar; cover and simmer for 30 minutes.

Add 4 dollops of brandy.

Serve on a bed of hot steaming rice smothered with the sauce.

Serves 4

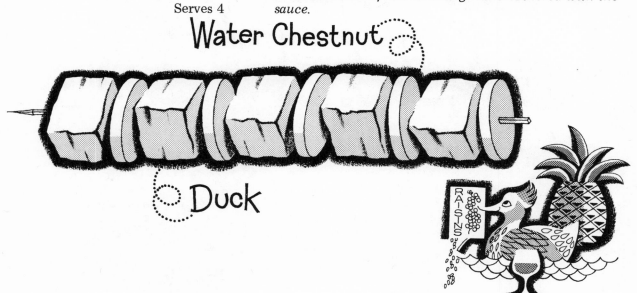

Water Chestnut

Duck

BROILED DUCK MANDARIN EN BROCHETTE

Duck (fresh or frozen)
Mandarin oranges, 11-ounce can
Honey
Soy sauce
Pepper, MSG
Paprika

Skin and bone a 3-pound duckling; retain as many large pieces of meat as possible.

Cut the meat into 1-inch chunks and thread on each of 4 bamboo skewers; alternate each piece of duck with a segment of mandarin orange.

Brush the skewers with a mixture of 3 parts honey and 1 part soy sauce; season with a sprinkle of pepper, MSG, and paprika.

Broil or barbeque under medium heat until golden brown.

Serve with French-cut green beans and thinly sliced tomatoes.

Serves 4

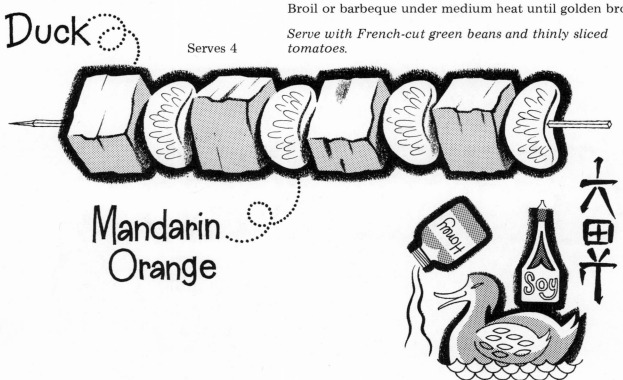

70

SKEWERED TURKEY BREAST WITH WALNUTS

Turkey breast
Pitted black olives
Flour
Egg
Finely chopped walnuts
Butter
Paprika
Dry white wine
Cornstarch
Parsley flakes

Skin and bone a 3-pound turkey breast; cut into 1-inch cubes.

Thread on each of 8 butcher skewers, alternating turkey and pitted black olives.

Dust the skewers with flour, dip in beaten egg, and roll skewers in finely chopped walnuts.

Sauté until golden brown in a mixture of ½ stick of butter and ½ teaspoon paprika.

Remove the skewers to a platter and add to the skillet 1 cup dry white wine mixed with 1 tablespoon cornstarch and ½ teaspoon parsley flakes. Return the skewers to the skillet and simmer for 30 minutes.

Sprinkle with additional chopped walnuts and serve on a bed of hot buttered noodles.

Serves 4

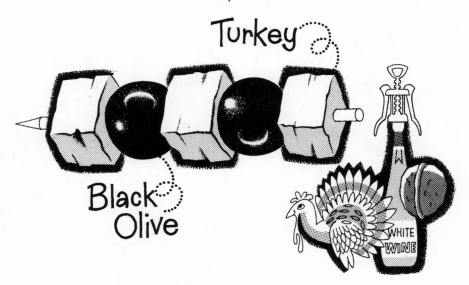

Turkey

Black Olive

WHITE WINE

SKEWERED CHICKEN LIVERS ALEXANDER

Chicken livers
Bamboo shoots, 6-ounce can
Canadian bacon, 1 pound chunk
Soy sauce
Dry red wine
Curry powder
Ginger

Slice 16 large chicken livers almost in two and carefully wrap each chunk around a small piece of bamboo shoot.

Thread on each of 4 thin bamboo skewers, securing the liver to the bamboo shoot.

Alternate the liver-bamboo shoots with 1-inch chunks of Canadian bacon.

Marinate the skewers in a shallow pan for 1 hour in the refrigerator in a mixture of ½ cup soy sauce, ½ cup wine, ¼ teaspoon curry powder, and ¼ teaspoon ginger.

Drain and broil or barbeque until the liver is tender. Baste occasionally with the marinade.

Serves 4   *Serve with hot steaming rice.*

Chicken Liver   Bamboo Shoot

Canadian Bacon

Soy

Curry Powder

BAMBOO SHOOTS

SKEWERED CHICKEN LIVERS SAUTÉED IN SHERRY AND BUTTER

Chicken livers
Fresh mushrooms
Butter
Purple onion
Cornstarch
Beef bouillon
Sherry
Salt, pepper, MSG
Chopped parsley

Alternate 1 pound chicken livers and 12 mushroom caps on 8 butcher skewers.

Sauté the skewers in ¼ stick of butter until lightly browned on all sides. Remove to a platter.

Add to the skillet diced mushroom stems, one small chopped purple onion, 1 tablespoon cornstarch thoroughly mixed with ½ cup beef bouillon, ½ cup sherry, ¼ teaspoon salt, ¼ teaspoon pepper, and ½ teaspoon MSG. Simmer until thickened.

Return the skewers to the skillet; add 1 tablespoon chopped parsley and heat until piping hot.

Serves 4

Serve on toast doused with a liberal serving of the sauce.

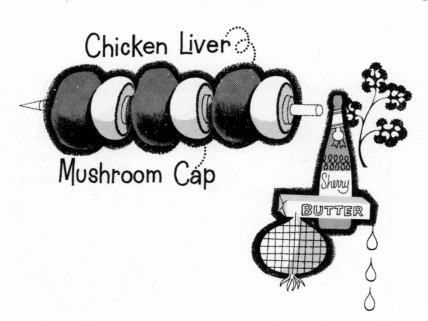

Chicken Liver

Mushroom Cap

Sherry

BUTTER

NUCI-NUCI

Chicken livers, 2 pounds
Water chestnuts, 8-ounce can
Bacon

Drain the liquid from a can of water chestnuts and slice each chestnut in half.

Wrap a slice of water chestnut and a chicken liver with a half slice of bacon and thread on each of 4 thin bamboo skewers.

Broil or barbeque until the bacon is crisp; turn frequently.

Serves 4

Serve with plum sauce and garnish with a generous scoop of hot steaming rice.

PLUM SAUCE

Pineapple preserves
Vinegar

Mix ½ cup pineapple preserves with ⅛ cup vinegar. Heat until mixture bubbles.

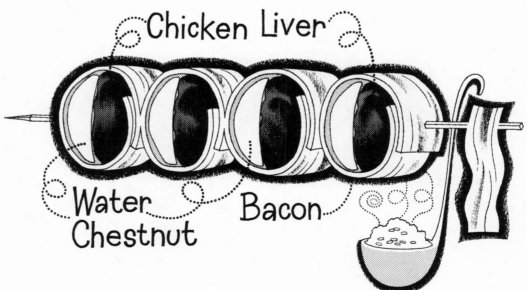

74

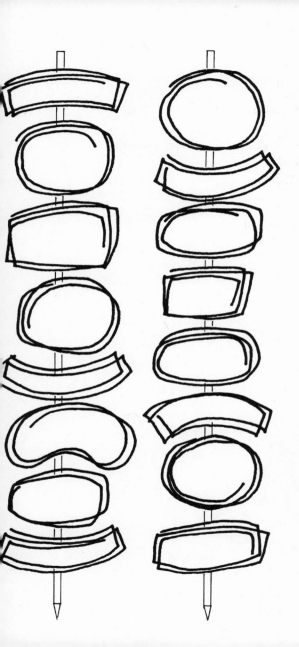

SEA FOOD

SEAFOOD SCRAMBLE ON SKEWERS

Trout, bass, or perch fillets
Shrimp
Clams
Scallops
Salt, pepper
Paprika, MSG
Prepared breading mix
Dijon mustard
Butter

Cut 1 pound of fish fillets into 8 square pieces.

Simmer 8 large shrimp in salted water for 10 minutes and drain, peel, and devein.

Steam 8 large clams in ¼ cup water in a covered pot until shells open; remove from shells.

Wash and dry 8 scallops.

Alternate 2 pieces of fish, 2 shrimp, 2 scallops, and 2 clams on each of 4 long bamboo skewers.

Add ¼ teaspoon salt, ¼ teaspoon fresh cracked pepper, ½ teaspoon paprika, and ½ teaspoon MSG to 1 cup of a prepared breading mix; roll the skewered seafood scramble in the mixture.

Dot the seafood with Dijon mustard and sauté on each side in 4 tablespoons butter until golden brown.

Garnish with parsley and lemon wedges and serve with French-cut green beans.

Serves 4

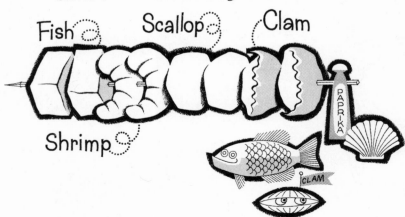

76

SKEWERED BASS IN BURGUNDY SAUCE

Bass fillets
Butter
Carrots
Onion
Garlic clove
Shallots (or green onion heads)
Salt, pepper, MSG
Dry white Burgundy

Cut 2 pounds of bass fillets into strips ¾-inch wide by about 2 inches long. Fold each strip in half and thread on 8 butcher skewers.

Sauté the following mixture in butter until golden brown: ½ cup finely chopped carrots, ½ cup minced onion, 1 finely chopped garlic clove, 4 chopped shallots, ½ teaspoon salt, ¼ teaspoon cracked pepper, and ½ teaspoon MSG.

Add the skewered fish and 2 cups dry white Burgundy wine to the skillet; cover and simmer for 20 minutes.

Serves 4   *Serve with hot Harvard beets.*

SKEWERED TROUT IN ANCHOVY SAUCE

Trout fillets
Fresh sweet red peppers or canned
    pimento
Eggs
Dry white wine
Cream
Flour
Cornmeal
Tarragon
Butter
Fresh garlic
Anchovies
Paprika

Cut 1½ pounds of trout fillets into strips about 3 inches long and 1 inch wide; fold in half and thread on each of 8 butcher skewers, alternating trout with 1-inch square pieces of sweet red pepper or pimento.

Dip the skewers in a mixture of 2 eggs lightly beaten with 1 tablespoon dry white wine and 1 tablespoon cream; coat the skewers with a mixture of 1 cup flour, 1 cup cornmeal, and a dash of chopped tarragon.

Sauté skewers in ½ stick butter together with 1 clove finely minced garlic.

Transfer the fish to a heated platter and add 4 minced anchovies, ½ cup dry white wine, and ½ teaspoon paprika to the skillet. Scrape the pan and simmer for 5 minutes.

Pour the wine sauce over the fish and serve immediately.

Garnish with watercress and serve with buttered asparagus tips.

Serves 4

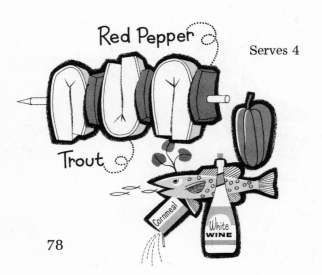

Red Pepper

Trout

Cornmeal

White WINE

MARINATED SHRIMP

Cooked shrimp, large
French dressing
Paprika
Celery seed

Marinate 16 cooked and cleaned large shrimp for 1 hour at room temperature in 1 cup prepared French dressing.

Thread the shrimp on each of 8 bamboo skewers.

Dust lightly with paprika and celery seed; broil or barbeque for 5 minutes on each side.

Appetizer for 4

Serve with squares of garlic toast.

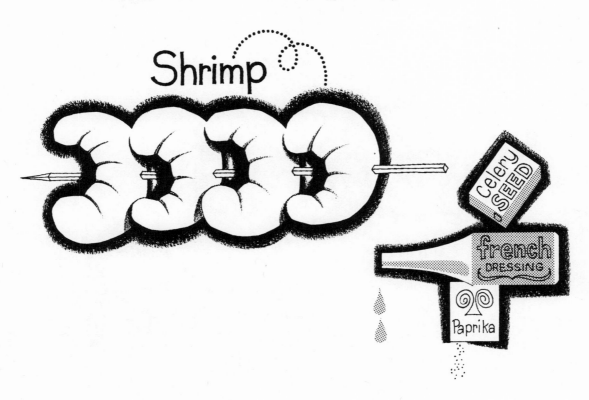

Shrimp

Celery SEED

french DRESSING

Paprika

PEPPERED SHRIMP EN BROCHETTE

Shrimp
Milk
Fresh cracked black pepper
White cornmeal
Green pepper
Butter

Place 2 pounds cooked and cleaned shrimp in a bowl and cover with milk containing ½ tablespoon fresh cracked pepper; marinate for 2 hours in the refrigerator.

Coat the shrimp with white cornmeal and thread the shrimp on each of 8 butcher skewers, alternating each shrimp with a 1-inch square of green pepper.

Sauté the skewered shrimp and peppers in ¼ stick of butter until golden brown on all sides.

Serves 4   *Serve with French-cut green beans.*

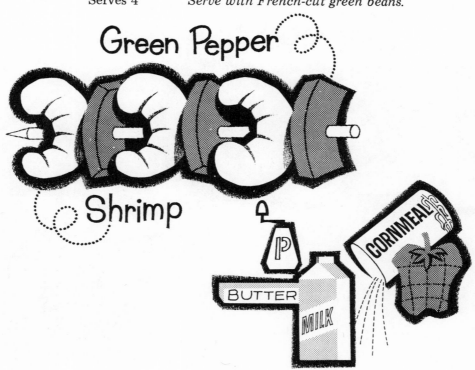

80

NEW ORLEANS SHRIMP BROCHETTES

Green pepper
Large shrimp
Dry white wine
Bread crumbs
Mayonnaise
Sour cream
Green onion
Salt, pepper, MSG
Paprika

Cut 2 green peppers into ¾-inch squares.

Alternate 1½ pounds cooked and cleaned shrimp with the pepper on each of 4 bamboo skewers.

Dampen the skewers in white wine and then dip in bread crumbs.

Arrange the skewers in a baking pan and cover with a blend of 1 cup mayonnaise, 1 cup sour cream, and 1 cup chopped green onions (heads and stems).

Dust with paprika and bake at 450° F. for 10 minutes.

Serves 4   *Serve with a fresh garden salad.*

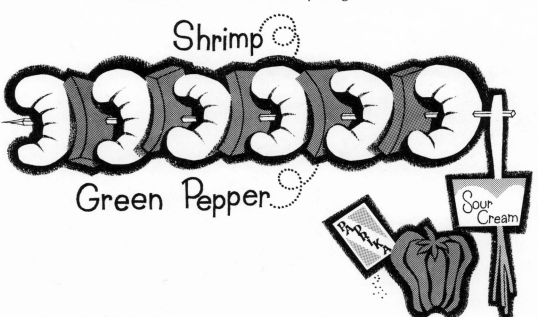

81

APRICOT SHRIMP CURRY

Dried apricots
Curry powder
Paprika
Butter
Cornstarch
Seasoned salt
Chicken bouillon
Egg yolk
Cream
Cognac
Shrimp, 16 large
Pimento, 4-ounce jar

Sauté ½ cup diced, dried apricots, ½ teaspoon curry powder, and ½ teaspoon paprika in ¼ stick of butter for 5 minutes; stir constantly.

Blend 1 tablespoon cornstarch, ¼ teaspoon seasoned salt, and 1 cup chicken bouillon; add to the skillet and simmer and stir until thickened.

Add to the skillet 1 egg yolk beaten lightly with ½ cup cream and ¼ cup Cognac.

Alternate the cooked and cleaned shrimp with small pimento squares on each of 8 butcher skewers; simmer in the sauce for 10 minutes.

Serve with a garnish of hot steaming rice, liberally doused with the sauce.

Serves 4

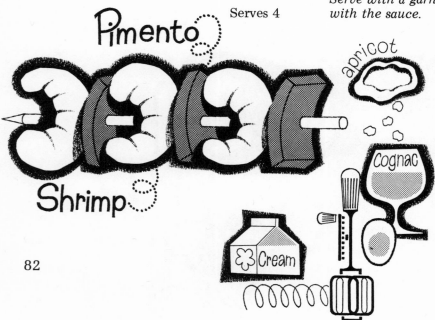

82

SHRIMP MOZZARELLA ON A STICK

Shrimp
Pitted black olives
Peanut oil
Mozzarella cheese
Bread crumbs

Thread 2 pounds of cooked and cleaned shrimp on each of 4 thin bamboo skewers; alternate each shrimp with a pitted black olive.

Brush the skewers with oil and broil or barbeque 5 minutes on each side.

Prior to serving, place a long strip of mozzarella cheese on each skewer and lightly dust with dry bread crumbs. Return to the broiler for a few minutes until the cheese just bubbles.

Serves 4   *Serve with hot buttered spaghetti.*

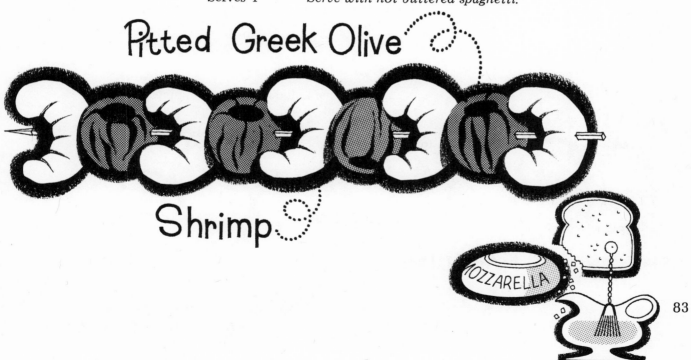

Pitted Greek Olive

Shrimp

83

PINEAPPLE AND LOBSTER ON SKEWERS

Lobster tails
Pineapple slices, 14-ounce can
Cayenne pepper
Chinese mustard
Olive oil

Cook 2 pounds of frozen lobster tails according to the directions on the package.

Cool and remove shells; cut lobster into 1-inch chunks.

Thread lobster chunks on each of four 8-inch bamboo skewers, alternating each chunk of lobster with 1-inch squares of canned sliced pineapple.

Dust lightly with cayenne pepper, brush with olive oil, dot with Chinese mustard, and broil or barbeque on all sides until golden brown.

Serves 4

Serve with a garnish of hot applesauce and shoestring potatoes. Down with a HAWAIIAN FOG.

HAWAIIAN FOG

Serves 4

Combine remaining pineapple juice, pineapple scraps, 4 ice cubes, and 8 ounces of vodka in a blender; mix and pour into chilled glasses.

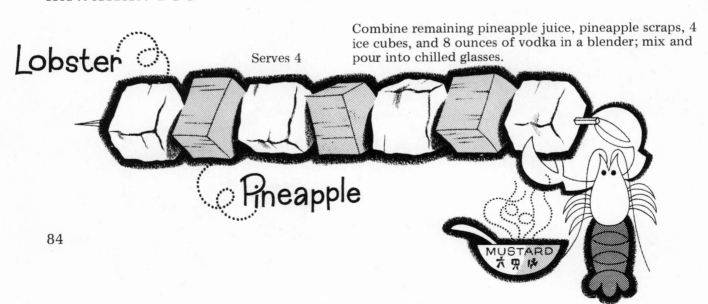

Lobster

Pineapple

MUSTARD

BROCHETTES OF LOBSTER WAIKIKI

Frozen lobster tails
Water chestnuts
Egg
Cornstarch
Salt
Peanut oil
Celery

Boil 4 large lobster tails according to the directions on the package. Cool and remove the lobster meat from the shell.

Finely mince the lobster and mix with ½ cup minced water chestnuts, 1 beaten egg, 1 teaspoon cornstarch, and ½ teaspoon salt. Form into 1-inch balls and sauté in ¼ cup hot oil in a heavy skillet until crusty.

Remove the balls from the skillet; cool slightly and thread on long bamboo skewers, alternating each lobster ball with a 1-inch chunk of celery.

Return the skewers to the skillet and sauté for 10 minutes; turn frequently.

Serves 4

Serve with hot buttered noodles lightly dusted with nutmeg.

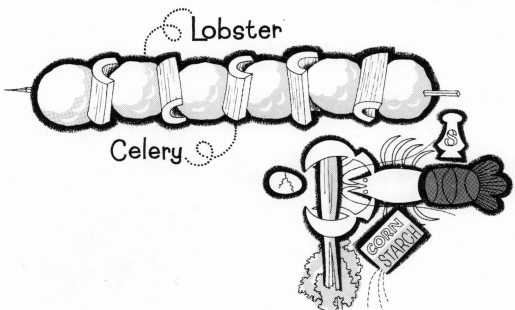

BROCHETTES OF ISLAND LOBSTER

Frozen lobster tails
Mushroom caps, 3-ounce jar
Pimento, 4-ounce jar
Fresh garlic
Ground pork
Peanut oil
Soy sauce
Ground ginger
Paprika
Flour
Beef bouillon

Boil 4 large lobster tails according to the directions on the package; cool and remove the lobster meat from the shell.

Cut the lobster meat into 1-inch chunks and thread on each of 4 long bamboo skewers; alternate each lobster chunk with a mushroom cap and a square of pimento.

Sauté 1 clove slivered garlic and ¼ pound ground pork in 2 tablespoons hot oil until browned and done.

Add to the skillet a mixture of 2 tablespoons soy sauce, 1 teaspoon ground ginger, ½ teaspoon paprika, 2 tablespoons flour, 2 cups beef bouillon; stir and simmer for 10 minutes.

Add the skewers to the skillet, cover, and simmer for 10 minutes.

Serves 4   *Serve on triangles of toast and drench with the sauce.*

Lobster   Pimento

Mushroom Cap

SKEWERED OYSTERS WITH BACON-CRAB SAUCE

Oysters, 24 (fresh or canned)
Bacon, 12 strips
Crab meat, 6½-ounce can
Port wine
Bread crumbs

Fry 4 strips of bacon until crisp; drain fat. Remove bacon, crumble, and return to the skillet.

Add 1 clove slivered garlic, ½ cup minced crab meat, and ½ cup port wine. Simmer for 10 minutes.

Thread the oysters on each of 8 butcher skewers and roll in bread crumbs.

Wrap each skewer with a strip of bacon and broil under moderate heat for 10 minutes.

Serve on toasted English muffins spooned over with the sauce.

Serves 4

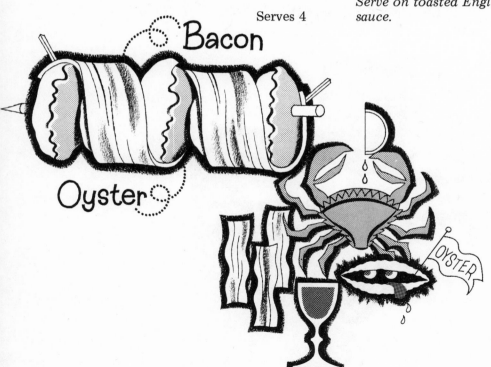

Bacon

Oyster

OYSTERS GOURMET

Oysters (fresh or canned)
Grated Parmesan cheese
Rye bread, unsliced
Eggs
Light cream
Bread crumbs
Butter

Pat dry 24 medium-sized oysters and roll in Parmesan cheese.

Alternate the coated oysters with 1-inch square slices of rye bread on each of 8 butcher skewers.

Dip the skewers in a mixture of 2 beaten eggs and 2 tablespoons cream; roll in bread crumbs.

Sauté the skewers in ½ stick of hot butter until golden brown.

Serves 4

Serve with a garnish of watercress and lemon wedges.

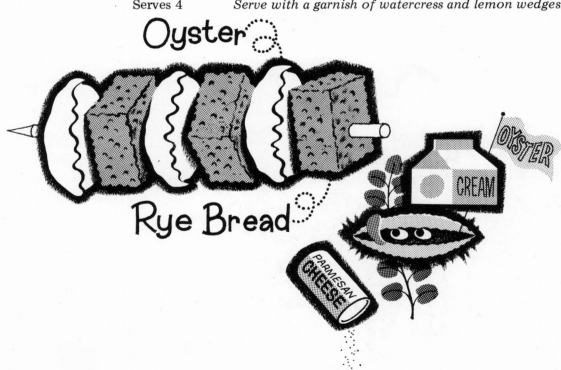

BROILED OYSTERS EN BROCHETTE

Stewing oysters (fresh or canned)
Martini onions
Butter
Fresh parsley
Allspice
Cayenne pepper
Bread crumbs
Lemon juice

Cook 2 dozen oysters in their own juice combined with 1 tablespoon butter until the edges curl.

Drain and thread the oysters on each of 4 long bamboo skewers; alternate each oyster with a small martini onion.

Sauté the skewered oysters and onions for about 10 minutes in a mixture of ¼ cup butter, ¼ cup chopped parsley, ⅛ teaspoon ground allspice, and ⅛ teaspoon cayenne pepper.

Place the skewers in a foil-lined broiling pan and spoon the sauce over the skewers. Dust with bread crumbs and sprinkle with lemon juice.

Broil until the oysters are lightly browned.

Serves 4   *Serve on a bed of lettuce with a garnish of lemon wedges.*

89

SKEWERED SMOKED OYSTERS

Smoked oysters, two 4-ounce cans
Soy sauce
Pepper
Paprika
Parsley flakes

Drain the oysters and marinate in ½ cup soy sauce for 15 minutes.

Thread the oysters on each of 8 short, thin bamboo skewers; season with pepper and paprika.

Dust the skewers with parsley flakes and broil for a few minutes.

Appetizer, serves 4

Smoked Oyster

90

SKEWERED SCALLOPS AMANDINE

Scallops
Milk
Salt, pepper
Flour
Black pitted olives
Butter
Blanched, slivered almonds

Dip the scallops in milk and then roll in flour seasoned with salt and pepper; thread the scallops on each of 8 butcher skewers; alternate scallops with pitted black olives.

Sauté the skewers in ½ stick of hot butter until golden brown on all sides.

Add ½ cup blanched, slivered almonds to the skillet and sauté for an additional 10 minutes.

Serves 4

Serve on a bed of hot steaming rice and cover with the almond butter sauce. Garnish with lemon wedges.

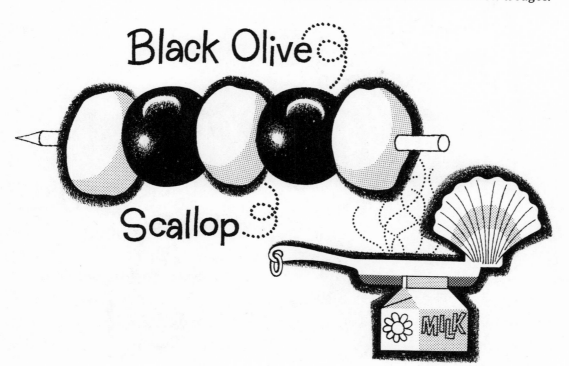

Black Olive

Scallop

91

MUSHROOMS AND SNAILS ON SKEWERS

Mushrooms, 24 whole fresh
Fresh parsley
Green onions
Salt
Cayenne pepper
Butter
Snails, 6-ounce can
Bread crumbs
Garlic juice

Prepare a sauce by sautéing the finely chopped mushroom stems, 1 teaspoon minced parsley, ½ cup diced green onions (heads and stems), ¼ teaspoon salt, and ⅛ teaspoon cayenne pepper in ½ stick of browned butter.

Alternate mushroom caps and snails on each of 4 bamboo skewers.

Arrange the skewers in a foil-covered broiling pan and spread the sauce over the skewers.

Sprinkle with bread crumbs, dot with garlic juice, and broil for 5 minutes.

Serves 4

Serve with a garnish of lemon wedges and parsley sprigs.

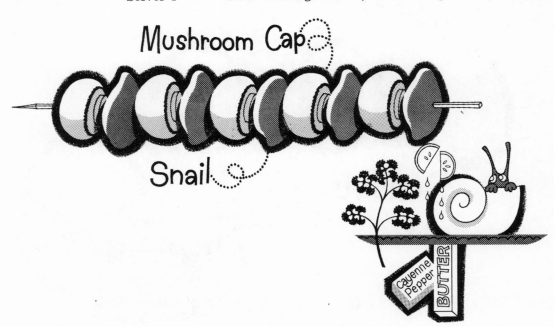

Mushroom Cap

Snail

92

STEAMED CLAMS MAXWELL HOUSE (UNSKEWERED)

Fresh Littleneck clams
Butter
Lemon juice

Scrub 4 dozen Littleneck clams and loosely sack in cheesecloth.

Add ½ cup water to a clean 3-pound coffee can and add the sack of clams. Make a cover of aluminum foil and tie around the can. Punch a small hole in the cover and place the coffee can on a grill over an open fire or on the stove. Boil for 10 minutes after the first steam spouts.

Serve with melted butter and lemon juice. Save the broth for drinking or clam dipping.

HIGH-IN-A-HURRY

Mix the hot clam broth with 8 ounces of vodka and pour into mugs. Add a dash of Worcestershire sauce and 2 drops of Tabasco sauce to each mug.

Serves 4

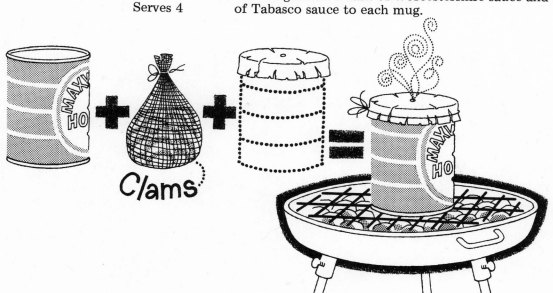

Clams

93

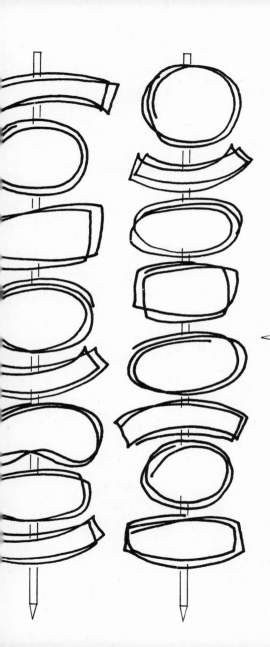

FRUITS & VEGETABLES

SKEWERED YOUNG CARROTS

Small young carrots
Salt
Garlic
Rosemary
Butter
Dried parsley flakes

Peel and then cut 1½ pounds of small young carrots into 1-inch chunks; parboil in salted water for 30 minutes.

Thread carrot chunks on each of 4 long bamboo skewers.

Blend one clove crushed garlic and ¼ teaspoon rosemary in 3 tablespoons melted butter.

Brush the carrots with a liberal amount of the seasoned butter and broil or grill until golden brown.

Serves 4

Dust with parsley flakes and serve steaming hot.

Carrot

BROILED CUCUMBERS

Cucumbers
Butter
Salt
Dried dill

Serves 4

Cut a large cucumber in half lengthwise, and then cut each half into ½-inch slices. Thread on each of 8 butcher skewers.

Brush with melted butter, sprinkle with salt and finely chopped dill, and broil for 2 or 3 minutes on both sides under moderate heat.

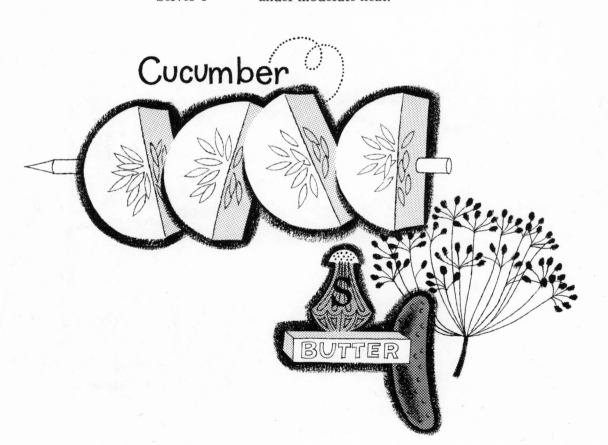

Cucumber

SKEWERED POTATOES

Small whole potatoes, 16-ounce can
Butter
Oregano
Onion powder
Paprika
Salt, pepper

Thread potatoes on each of 4 bamboo skewers.

Brush the skewered potatoes with 3 tablespoons melted butter seasoned with ¼ teaspoon oregano, ¾ teaspoon onion powder, ¼ teaspoon paprika, and a dash of salt and pepper.

Broil the skewers until brown crusty spots appear; turn frequently and brush occasionally with the seasoned butter.

Serves 4

Garnish with crushed parsley before serving.

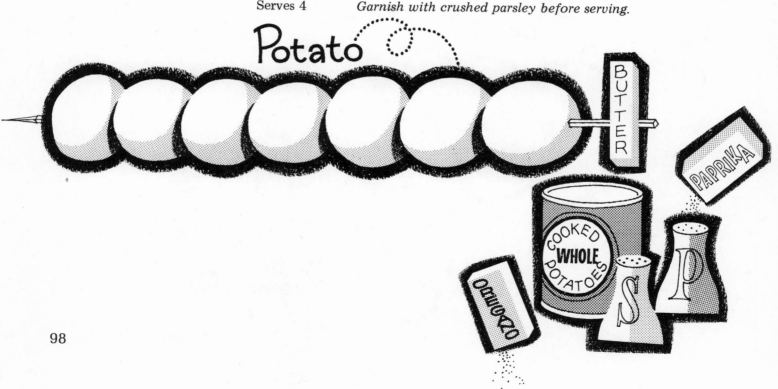

BROILED TOMATOES ON A STICK

Cherry tomatoes
Olive oil
Bread crumbs
Parsley flakes

Serves 4

Place 3 firm cherry tomatoes on each of 4 butcher skewers.

Brush with olive oil, dust with bread crumbs and parsley flakes, and broil for 5 minutes.

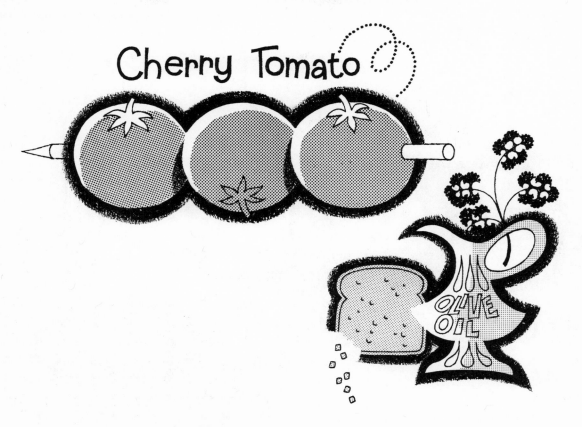

Cherry Tomato

TURNIPS AND PEPPERS DIANE

Fresh turnips
Green peppers
Butter
Parsley
Garlic salt

Parboil 2 medium-sized peeled turnips for 30 minutes; cool and cut into 1-inch cubes.

Cut 2 sweet green peppers into 1-inch squares.

Alternate peppers and turnips on each of 4 butcher skewers and sauté in 4 tablespoons butter until lightly browned.

Serves 4

Sprinkle with parsley and ¼ teaspoon garlic salt and serve steaming hot.

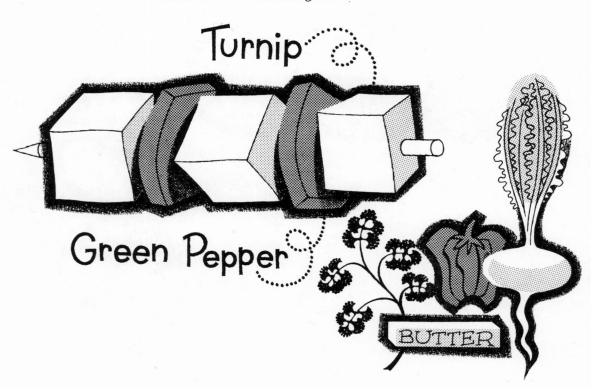

Turnip

Green Pepper

BUTTER

EGGPLANT ERNESTINE EN BROCHETTE

Eggplant
Pitted black olives, 8-ounce can
Prepared French dressing

Peel a large eggplant and cut into 1-inch cubes.

Thread on each of 4 butcher skewers, alternating the eggplant with a pitted black olive.

Marinate the skewers in French dressing for ½ hour at room temperature. Drain and broil or barbeque until tender, but not too soft.

Serves 4

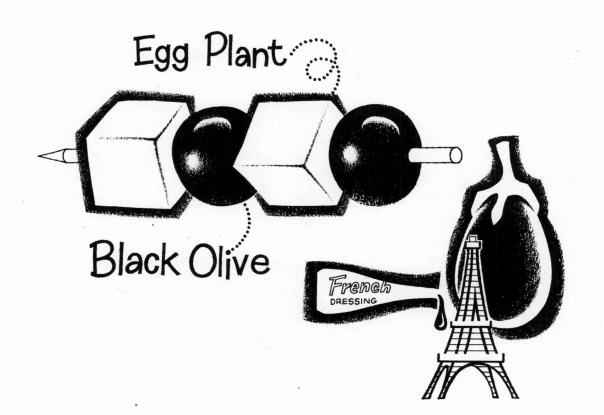

Egg Plant

Black Olive

French DRESSING

101

FRUIT FONDUE

Bananas
Pineapple
Cherries, 16-ounce can
Lemon juice
Semi-sweet chocolate bits
Corn oil

Slice 2 bananas into ½-inch discs and brush with lemon juice, cut 4 pieces of sliced pineapple into 8 segments each, and drain the juice from a can of dark sweet cherries.

Alternate the fruit on butcher skewers, leaving 1½ inches free at the end of the skewer for handling.

Lay the skewers on wax paper and place in the freezer for about an hour or until frozen.

Prepare a hot chocolate sauce by melting 1 package of semi-sweet chocolate bits with 3 tablespoons cooking oil in a chafing dish. Carefully add additional oil if necessary to bring the chocolate to a syrupy consistency.

Serves 4

Dip the frozen skewered fruit into the chocolate sauce, swirl around, and eat off the stick.

Banana

Pineapple

Sweet Cherry

Semi-Sweet CHOCOLATE

102

YUMMY RUMMY SKEWERED FRUIT

Bananas
Fresh peach
Orange
Cinnamon sugar
White rum

Slice 2 bananas into ¾-inch discs, cut a peach into chunks, and break an orange into segments.

Alternate slices of bananas, chunks of peaches, and orange segments on butcher skewers.

Sauté in butter until lightly browned on all sides.

Sprinkle with cinnamon sugar; carefully warm three tablespoons white rum in a sauce pan, ignite, and pour over the skewered fruit.

Serves 4

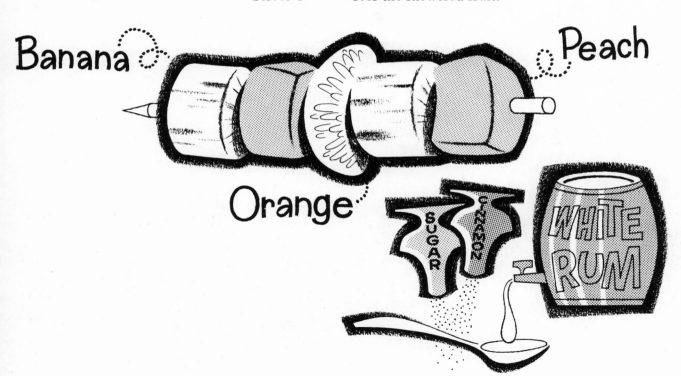

Banana

Peach

Orange

SUGAR CINNAMON

WHITE RUM

ORANGES DOMINICAN EN BROCHETTE

Oranges
Red and green Maraschino cherries
Dry red wine
Sugar
Ground cloves
Cinnamon

Peel 4 large oranges and break into segments; discard the seeds and other tissue.

Thread on butcher skewers, alternating 2 orange segments with a red and then a green Maraschino cherry.

In a sauce pan blend and heat ⅓ cup dry red wine, 2½ tablespoons sugar, ⅛ teaspoon ground cloves, and a dash of cinnamon.

Pour the wine sauce over the skewered oranges, chill, and serve.

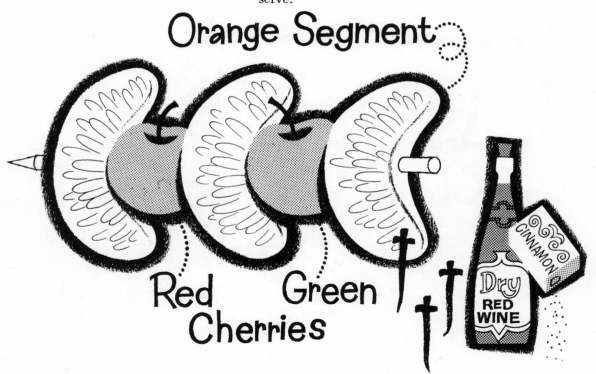

Orange Segment

Red Green
Cherries

Dry RED WINE

CINNAMON

BROCHETTES OF MIXED FRUIT

Fresh strawberries
Fresh pineapple
Orange segments
Mozzarella cheese
Flour
Salt
Egg
Milk
Powdered sugar
Cinnamon
Oil

Serves 4

Alternate strawberries, 1-inch cubes of pineapple, orange segments, and 1-inch cubes of mozzarella cheese on each of 4 bamboo skewers.

Dust with flour and then dip into a batter consisting of ½ cup flour, ½ teaspoon salt, 1 beaten egg, and just enough milk to thin to a creamy consistency.

Fry the brochettes in deep oil until brown. Remove from oil and dust with a mixture of powdered sugar and cinnamon.

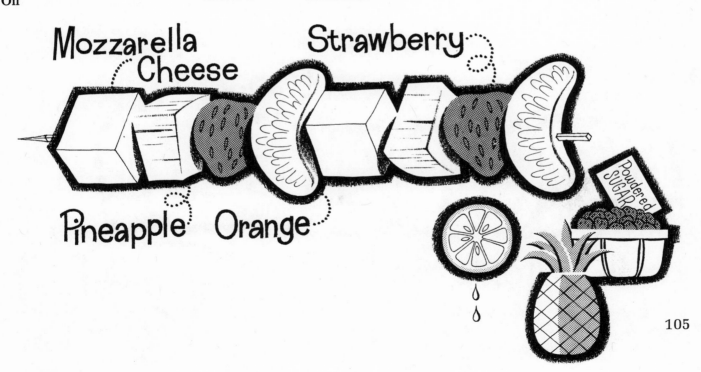

SKEWERED B & B (BANANAS AND BACON)

Bananas
Bacon
Apple
Powdered sugar
Cognac

Peel 3 firm bananas and slice into 1-inch discs.

Wrap a piece of bacon around the circumference of each banana slice, overlap, and fasten with a toothpick.

Peel and cut an apple into ¼-inch slices and then cut each slice into 1-inch squares. Alternate the bacon-wrapped bananas and apple squares on each of 4 long bamboo skewers.

Broil for 5 minutes on each side, or until the bacon is crisp. The apple squares will keep the skewers from rolling.

Dust with powdered sugar and pour flaming Cognac over the skewers at the time of serving.

Serves 4

Bacon

Banana

Apple

106

GARLIC SOUP

Cream of celery soup, two 15-ounce cans
Fresh garlic
Water
Sherry wine
Cornstarch

Add 4 cloves finely chopped garlic to two cans cream of celery soup prepared according to the directions on the can.

Add ¼ cup sherry and ½ tablespoon cornstarch blended with a little water to the soup, and simmer for an additional 20 minutes.

Strain through cheesecloth and discard the solids.

Serves 4

Serve with warm, buttered French bread.

107

DILL SOUP

Cream of celery soup, two 15-ounce cans
Dried dill
Sherry wine
Cornstarch
Cucumber

Add 1 teaspoon of crushed dill to two cans cream of celery soup, and prepare the soup according to the directions on the can.

Add ¼ cup sherry and ½ tablespoon cornstarch mixed with a little water to the soup, and simmer for 20 minutes.

Strain through cheesecloth and discard the solids.

Float 2 thin cucumber slices on each serving.

Serves 4

Serve with warm French bread and butter.

108

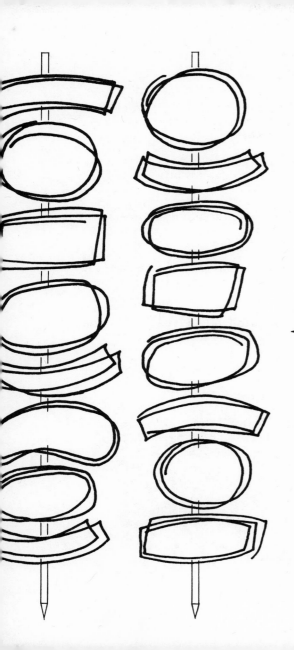

ODDS & ENDS

SKEWERING-UP AN OUTDOOR STOVE

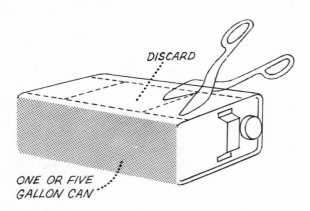

DISCARD

ONE OR FIVE
GALLON CAN

A half-hour's worth of cutting and bending on a clean five-gallon oil can will produce a picnic stove that can handle 4 long metal skewers.

Punch a starter hole near the center of one of the sides; with tin snips or heavy shears cut the can as shown in the figure.

Bend the flaps upward and notch them; the notches should be cut just wide enough to hold a square metal skewer and prevent it from turning.

Coat hangers, straightened out and rebent as shown, form the legs. Four small holes punched with a nail will support these legs.

Line the can with aluminum foil, add a layer of charcoal, ignite, and you are ready to skewer-up a meal.

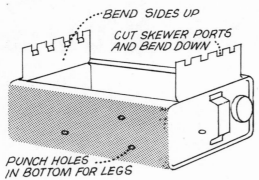

BEND SIDES UP

CUT SKEWER PORTS
AND BEND DOWN

PUNCH HOLES
IN BOTTOM FOR LEGS

COAT HANGERS

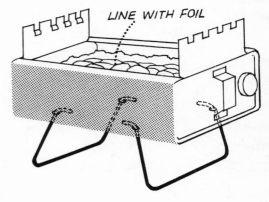

LINE WITH FOIL

A HIBACHI FIT FOR SKEWERING

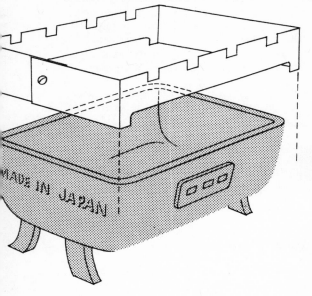

With a little sheet metal and a little effort, a hibachi stove or even an old roasting pot can be fitted for skewering. A piece of sheet metal an inch and a half wide, short or long as the case may be, is notched and bent to fit the stove or roaster, as shown. If square skewers are used, the notches should be just wide enough to prevent the skewers from turning. By eliminating the grate, clean up is easy.

SKEWERING IN A ROASTER or a hot time in the old "pot" tonight

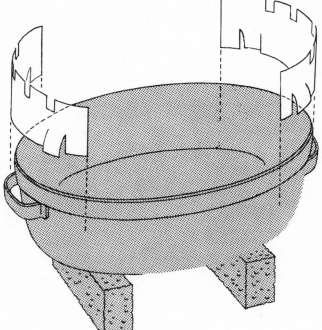

111

HERBS, SPICES, AND IDEAS

With a touch of courage you can spark up and add variation to your recipes or sauces. A sparing touch of this or that will change the entire character of the dish—a typically French flavor is transformed to East Indian—Chinese to Hungarian. Tread lightly, though; a little spice or a pinch of herbs goes a long way—and stick to one highly seasoned dish per meal.

ALLSPICE
: Imparts an Oriental flavor; crack two whole allspice and add to marinades; drop one or two whole allspice in the skillet for those sautéed dishes.

ANISE SEED
: Originally from southern Europe; a pinch or two is delightful with seafood.

ARROWROOT
: Gourmet-style thickener for sauces and gravies; neutral taste.

BASIL
: French and Italian heritage; a grand accompaniment for those conglomerations containing tomatoes; ¼ teaspoon is sufficient for recipes serving four.

BAY LEAVES
: Add an Italian flavor to sauces and gravies; add one or two to your marinades; add one or two to skillet sauces.

CARAWAY SEED
: Of Dutch descent; after cooking, sprinkle over dishes containing ham or pork; imparts a unique nut-like flavor to cooked sauces.

CARDAMON
: Imported originally from India; add a dash of ground cardamon to meat sauces while simmering; adds a delicate sweet flavor.

CAYENNE PEPPER
: Much hotter than regular pepper; use sparingly in sauces for seafood, meat, and poultry to give a Mexican or Spanish touch.

112

CELERY SEED	A must in French cooking; adds a delightful flavor to sauces containing tomatoes and green peppers; use whole or ground.
CHERVIL	Adds a pungent flavor to cooked vegetables and fish sauces.
CHILI POWDER	A must for everything Mexican; carefully add a light dash to seafood sauces.
CINNAMON	A spice from the East Indies; adds a zesty taste to sauces; particularly good with duck and wild game.
CURRY	A mixture of Eastern herbs and spices imported from India; may be sparingly used in almost any recipe for that Eastern taste and aroma.
DILL	A plant of the carrot family; succulent aroma that beautifully blends with garlic in any recipe; fine garnish for soups and salads.
FENNEL	A classic herb from the parsley family; particularly good in Spanish and Italian dishes.
FENUGREEK	A product of Morocco and used in dishes of Greek origin; may be substituted for curry.
GINGER	From the tropics—Jamaica and the British West Indies; used with soy sauce for that Oriental touch for chicken, pork, lamb, or beef.
HICKORY SMOKED SALT	A sprinkle-on type of seasoning that can be added before cooking to impart a wood-smoke flavor.
HORSERADISH	For a sensational taste, sliver fresh horseradish into curls just as you would carrots and use as a garnish for beef; a tongue-tingling treat.

JUNIPER BERRIES	A basic ingredient of gin; try a few berries, crushed or whole, in your marinades for an interesting taste.
MARJORAM	Herb of the mint family of France; goes particularly well in lamb marinades; add a sprinkle as a garnish for your rice accompaniments.
MINT	An aromatic and flavorful herb; like marjoram, a dash of mint will enhance your hot steaming rice.
NUTMEG	A spice from the East Indies and a favorite in Swedish sauces. Buy the whole pods and freshly grate as needed—it's worth the effort just for the delicious aroma.
OREGANO	A must for the Mexican and Italian flavor; can be added during or after cooking to practically any recipe.
PAPRIKA	A mild, red condiment ground from the fruit of various peppers; use a colorful dash on salads and vegetables; add to oil when skillet browning.
POPPY SEED	An Asian herb with a nut-like flavor and odor. Lightly sprinkle over rice or baked potato for a surprisingly good taste.
ROSEMARY	Fresh and sweet, but packs a wallop, so use sparingly; goes well with sauces containing garlic.
SAFFRON	From the Mediterranean; one of the highest priced flavorings. Fortunately, a little goes a long, long way. A true gourmet seasoning for fish sauces, curry, and boiled rice.
SAGE	Grown in Dalmatia; this herb has a spicy aroma and can be used sparingly to perk up fowl, fish, and pork.

SAVORY	Fragrant Spanish herb; lends a delightful flavor to meat sauces, particularly those for lamb and veal.
SESAME SEED	Oriental heritage; toasted seed makes a great sprinkle-on garnish for vegetables and rice. Add to fish sauces for an interesting change. To toast, spread seeds in a pan, heat in 350° oven for 10 minutes; shake occasionally.
TARRAGON	An excellent addition to meat sauces, salad greens, and hot vegetables.
THYME	Use alone or with other herbs for a taste sensation; adapts well to seafood marinades and sauces.

INDEX

Major ingredients, those that end up on the skewers, and the method of cooking are listed along with the name of each recipe.

POULTRY RECIPES

SEAFOOD RECIPES

FRUIT AND VEGETABLE RECIPES

ODDS AND ENDS